MW00463805

## PRAISE FOR
### Living Earth Devotional

*"I treasure books like this one, which help you to see and think in new ways, continually pushing you out of your comfort zone and into more joy and wisdom than ever before. What better way to spend a year than with 365 ways of harmonizing with Gaia?"*

• • • • • •

Tess Whitehurst,
author of *Magical Housekeeping*
and *The Good Energy Book*

*"With this beautiful little guide to living green spirituality, Clea Danaan has given us a constant companion that can help us, every day of the year, to reconnect with that which is our birthright: our sense of belongingness in the great web of life on Earth."*

• • • • • •

Marian Van Eyk McCain,
editor of *GreenSpirit: Path to a New Consciousness*

# Living Earth

DEVOTIONAL

Dawn Alexander

CLEA DANAAN (Colorado) has been gardening organically for over twenty years. Her articles on ecology and spirituality have appeared in *SageWoman*, *Witches & Pagans*, *GreenSpirit*, and *Organic Family* magazines. She is the author of *Sacred Land*, *Voices of the Earth*, and *The Way of the Hen*. Her background in Reiki, expressive arts therapies, outdoor education, and somatic psychology inform her integrated and ecumenical writings.

365 GREEN PRACTICES
FOR SACRED CONNECTION

# *Living Earth*

## DEVOTIONAL

# CLEA DANAAN

*Llewellyn Publications*
WOODBURY, MINNESOTA

FIRST EDITION
First Printing, 2013

Book design and edit by Rebecca Zins
Cover credits: iStockphoto.com/14017308/Denys Fonchykov,
    15552617/spxChrome; SuperStock/1538R-69041/IMAGEZOO
Cover design by Ellen Lawson
Interior floral composition from *Ornamental Flowers, Buds and Leaves* by
    V. Ruprich-Robert (Dover, 2010); leaf from *922 Decorative Vector
    Ornaments CD-ROM & Book* (Dover, 2009)

Llewellyn Publications is a registered trademark of Llewellyn Worldwide Ltd.

Library of Congress Cataloging-in-Publication Data
The Cataloging-in-Publication Data for *Living Earth Devotional* is pending.
ISBN 978-0-7387-3658-7

Llewellyn Publications
A Division of Llewellyn Worldwide Ltd.
2143 Wooddale Drive
Woodbury, MN 55125-2989
www.llewellyn.com

Printed in the United States of America

# CONTENTS

# Introduction

I recently asked a group of people why they sought a deeper intuitive connection with nature. They all spoke of having lost their once-trusted connection to their intuition. They found solace and beauty in the natural world, and had a sense of nature's sentience and power, but they didn't know how to tap into this consciousness or trust what arose when they did connect. They longed for connection and understanding.

Many people also wonder how we can begin to heal the damage we've caused to our planet. We know climate change is real, but it feels so overwhelming and out of the average person's control. A little part of us might even wonder if living green is even worth it in the face of such destruction and the power of big oil.

This book offers creative solutions to these questions: how to attune with the natural world, what to do once you hear the voice of the earth, and not only *why* saving the sacred earth matters, but little ways in which you can help every day. To help you attune with the natural rhythms of the earth both practically and spiritually—and to know what to do with that attunement—this book guides you through 365 activities for living green spirituality. The activities are organized by the Wheel of the Year.

The Wheel of the Year is a series of eight holidays, or sabbats, practiced in Celtic and Wiccan spirituality. The sabbats are the solstices and equinoxes plus the four holidays at cross-quarters with those solar-based dates. There is a sabbat every six to six-and-a-half weeks. They mark the seasons—the journey of the earth around the sun. When you live each day attuned to these rhythms, your life is grounded in the earth and its place in the cosmos. You return to the Source. You find that nature is a bridge to Spirit, and that nature and Spirit both bring

you straight to your own soulwork. Nature, Spirit, and soul form a great Celtic knot of awakening and sacred living.

The daily practices in this book are designed to weave together all these integral pieces: nature, soul, purpose, creativity, earth, Spirit. They include journaling, simple crafts, meditation, a few prayers, activism, and ideas for a life centered in green spirituality. They are designed for personal spiritual discovery and for deepening your relationship with the earth *and* with each other.

We will play and pray with nature from a variety of angles. For practices designed to connect deeply with nature, I draw on nature-based spirituality, perma-culture and organic gardening, mystical Christianity, expressive arts, awareness practices, outdoor education, and plain old *play*. Earth-centered spirituality is not nec-essarily tied to any one religion. It is heart-centered and focused on aware, sacred living. It is internal and pri-vate, and it also calls one to action in the world, a bal-ance of inner and outer work. We will touch on all of these approaches.

The seasons and what is occurring at each sabbat will differ depending on where you live. I grew up in the Pacific Northwest and now live in arid Colorado, so my bias tends toward these climates. If you need to adapt an activity to fit where you live, please do so. You may want to mark an activity to come back to later, when the weather matches its theme or when you feel ready to tackle it. The point isn't to follow exactly what I've written but to apply spiritual and practical practices to what is actually happening where you live. The activities are made to be done in city, suburban, or wilderness areas. The natural world is everywhere. If you can escape to the mountains or the beach for a weekend, great, but it's not necessary for these activities.

You need not begin at Samhain (Halloween) but can begin the activities whenever you like. Proceed from wherever you begin. You can work with a group or alone, or a combination of these.

You will need a journal, a place for reflection and observation. I encourage drawing as well as writing.

For the craft and art projects, don't stress about artistic ability; just have fun. It's between you and the Divine and is about discovery. Meditations can be done quietly by yourself, read aloud, or even turned into rituals and acted out.

Adapt the activities to your style and needs. Not all of these activities will appeal to you, and some may push you into uncomfortable territory, like singing or making art or volunteering with others in need. Give them a try, and see what happens. There's no test and no shame. If you face physical challenges, you may need to adapt some of the activities; dance in whatever way you dance. All are welcome here.

When we come together as humans on a shared planet, as souls manifested at this time on this earth, we can make change. We can grow as people. We can reshape the relationship our species has with the land, the animals, the water, and the air.

Let us begin.

# Samhain

Samhain, celebrated as Halloween in the secular world, is the witch's New Year. The myth of Samhain is that the Goddess enters the Underworld and confronts the Lord of Death and Rebirth. In other traditions, the God enters the Underworld and the Goddess becomes a wise crone. The energy of the sabbat is about entering the dreamtime, the sacred womb or cave, and dancing with the transformative darkness. In temperate regions, all has been harvested from the garden and stored away for the coming winter. The woodpile is stacked high. We turn inward, secure in our homes against the cold and darkness. In contemporary society, we begin to think about and plan for the upcoming holidays. This time of year is about telling stories and handing down traditions. We honor our ancestors and invite their guidance as we continue to journey in the manifest world.

# October 31

Samhain is about death and release—letting go of what has been as we prepare for the rebirth of light at Yule. J. J. Bachofen wrote, "Without death, no rejuvenation is possible ... the positive power cannot for one moment exist without the negative power. Death, then, is not the opposite but the helper of life."[1] To move forward in your own life, you must let go of and make peace with the past; you must let that old part of you die.

Weather permitting, go outside and look for examples of death: dried leaves, shriveled berries, bones, etc. Sit with the things you have collected, and ask them for a message. Let feelings and images arise in you. Gently bring to mind something in your past that you must let go of in order to move forward into your fullest self. How does the message of these symbols guide you? Write about your experience in your journal.

# November 1

Go on a walk today, no matter what the weather is like. Dress appropriately, and stay out for as long as you are comfortable. Pay attention. Walk slowly. Listen and look. What animals and insects are out today? What are they doing? Sense them by expanding your bubble of awareness, and see what images and feelings you get. What are the trees doing? In many climates they will be pulling energy downward, into their roots. Can you match this energy in your body? If feeling energy is new to you, just focus on your five senses. What is the light like today? Where is the sun on the horizon? Is it windy, raining, snowing, clear? Close your eyes a moment, and feel how your body responds to the light and the weather. Record your observations in your journal, including any questions you have at this time, or draw what you have experienced.

## November 2

Today is All Souls' Day and the Day of the Dead, or *el Día de los Muertos*. A common image associated with this day, as well as with Samhain and Halloween, is the skeleton. Lie down, preferably on the earth (indoors is fine). Close your eyes, and bring your awareness to your bones. Feel their weight. Living bones are slightly flexible and very strong. Feel energy running along the lines of your bones. Feel the earth beneath you; become aware of the minerals in the earth. Feel your bones' minerals resonate with the earth's minerals. Spend some time feeling the connection between your skeleton and the stony earth.

# November 3

> *Only by understanding the dark side of the moon can we appreciate the light and not take it for granted. Only by facing the shadows of ourselves—the nasty little hidden corners that we fear—can we be complete.*
> • • • • • •
> Dianne Sylvan[2]

Go outside, and find a tree that gives you a sense of healing and strength. Ask the tree if it is open to helping you heal. If you get a sense of welcome, sit with your back against the tree's trunk, your sit bones firmly on the ground. If it's raining or snowing, you can do this indoors as a meditation, but do come back to the practice later outside with a living tree.

Breathe. Let your awareness spread into the tree and the earth. Feel the tree stretch high above and deep below. Let one of your shadows, the darker parts of yourself that seek healing, rise into your awareness.

Gently hold this shadow in the support and strength of the tree. Let the tree help you face your shadow. Notice the great power of the tree and its lack of judgment, fear, or condemnation. Sit with the great tree spirit for as long as you need to.

# November 4

The sun rests low on the horizon, and the days are short. The wind blows chilly, tossing up dry leaves. If you're like me, you crave warming soups and hearty bread. Concentrated foods and root vegetables thicken the blood in preparation for cooler weather. Sour foods like pickles, olives, and sourdough bread help organize and condense energy that has been scattered by the previous warmer seasons. Cooking with less water at lower heat and for longer times (hello, slow cooker!) helps internalize your focus, one of the tasks of autumn.[3] Make a stew in your slow cooker of locally grown root vegetables and hearty greens like kale (a pot on the stove is fine if you don't have a slow cooker). Add a gentle dose of salt for its grounding properties. Serve with sourdough bread and something fermented and tangy. Give thanks to the earth for her gifts, and feel how nourishing it is to eat with the energy of the season.

# November 5

This time of year we honor our ancestors. If you haven't already, dig a little (or a lot) into your family history. Family trees, photo albums, interviews of older relatives, and even genetic mapping can offer a lot of information about who came before you. As you study your ancestors and review what you already know, consider the land they lived on. Climate shapes who we are, what we value, and who we become. Weather and terrain affected your family's emigration, diet, and values. How has the land shaped your family? Were your ancestors herders or farmers? Did they relocate to be near water or in response to disasters like the Dust Bowl or Hurricane Katrina? Write about how these earthy influences have contributed to who you are today, including what you value, childhood experiences, and your ethnicity.

# November 6

Today, a meditation.

Imagine you are walking in a forest at dusk. A light breeze whispers through dry oak leaves and sets fir boughs gently swaying. You look up at where the crescent of the waning moon peeks back at you. Against the sky you see the flitting shapes of bats. You feel a shiver of excitement run down your spine.

The forest pathway curves downhill and eventually enters the dark mouth of a cave. You enter the darkness, feeling the cooler air on your face. You walk into the cave, knowing you are welcome and safe. The darkness envelops you. You feel supported and held by the cool dark.

Let the cave speak to you. What does it have to say? What lessons can the darkness offer you at this time?

# November 7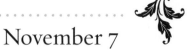

Take the messages you received from the natural symbols of death (October 31) and the cave (yesterday), as
well as any dream images or insights that have arisen
over the past week. Write or draw these messages on
small pieces of paper. Go outside and find a tree that
has lost its leaves. Nestle the words and images in holes
or crevices in the tree. Ask the tree if it will help you
in your journey of awakening. Some other natural being
besides a tree is also fine, like a stone outcropping or
another plant. Notice what happens now and over the
next few weeks. Pay attention to your dreams, another
way Spirit speaks to us. Record any messages from the
trees or your dreams in your journal.

# November 8

Many traditional cultures created lodges or huts for introspection and reflection at appropriate times. In tribal Jewish cultures, the red tent was a place to menstruate, rest, and rebuild sacred energy. A Native American death lodge was a place to face your own death, reflecting on who you are, facing your demons, and preparing for the future. Today many people find rejuvenation in the candlelit quiet of a church.

Make a lodge for yourself. Spend time there alone when you need to. This might be a chair in a dark corner that you smudge with a little white sage, a temporary cave made with a blanket over chairs like you did when you were a child, or even simply a weekly ritual of an herbal facial steam with a towel over your head. Go to your lodge regularly to reconnect with stillness and your true self.

# November 9

*Each night dream represents our brief descent into the Great Underdream, a dipping of our toes into the soulstream, a briefing on one or two points about the deeper life waiting and longing to be lived.*
Bill Plotkin, *Soulcraft*[4]

Do you have a recurring dream or a place you visit in your dreams? Describe them in your journal. Also write about the first night dreams you remember from your childhood. What images arise? Are there any animals, allies, trees, or landscapes that speak to you? Many of us return to the same dream landscape. Describe it. What do these dreams say about your life path, soul purpose, and the life you long to live?

# November 10

Birds often represent teachings from the Underworld or spirit realm, as they live on both the land and in the air. Some birds, in particular, offer teachings about the dreamtime, transitions, and exploring the darkness. These include the blackbird, who sings at the in-between time of twilight; owls and other nocturnal birds who can see in the darkness; and ravens and crows, who are dark, cunning, and intelligent. Weather permitting, go outside and look for birds. Find a fallen feather and sit in meditation with it, asking for guidance and giving thanks. Let the birds' message remind you that you, too, are of both the physical and spiritual worlds. For information on the medicine or teachings of any birds you encounter, see Ted Andrews' *Animal Speak*; *The Druid Animal Oracle* by Philip Carr-Gomm, Stephanie Carr-Gomm, and Bill Worthington; or *The Healing Wisdom of Birds* by Lesley Morrison.

# November 11

In different climates, leaves fall from the trees at different times. Notice which trees are losing or have lost their leaves now. Who is completely bare? Who holds on to crisp, dry leaves? Do some of the trees where you live still have their leaves? Even in a temperate climate that doesn't really experience autumn, trees drop leaves to make room for new growth. Notice the rhythms of your area. Pick a tree that calls to you. Listen to the tree, noticing its place in the environment.

On a spiritual level, trees connect earth to sky, moving vast amounts of water back and forth between these realms. They turn fire—the sun—into life. They are part of complex living communities above and below ground. They can inspire us to live more connected, flowing lives. To find the energy of the tree you chose, see *Flower and Tree Magic* by Richard Webster or *Tree Medicine, Tree Magic* by Ellen Evert Hopman.

# November 12

Choose someone no longer living who was passionate about a cause. Take action today in honor of this person's passion. For instance, my father was deeply concerned about global warming even before it was a popular movement. Today I might donate a small amount of money to a nonprofit organization focused on climate change, like 350.org. Or I might leave my lights off all day and not run the clothes dryer or oven. Or I might ride my bike instead of driving. I could also offset my carbon footprint by purchasing wind power or solar power credits at my electric company. In what way can you take action in honor of a loved one who is with us no longer?

# November 13

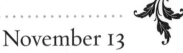

In many temperate regions, the season's first snow falls at this time of year. Go outside, and let snowflakes fall onto your upturned face. Your inner warmth melts them quickly. As the earth chills outside, we snuggle into blankets and cradle warm mugs of tea. We turn inward. When you come in from playing in the snow, stir a spoonful of snow into your tea, literally taking in the cold weather. Close your eyes as your tea warms you. Feel the energy pulsing inside your body. Give a prayer of thanks for the water cycle that brings us both snow and mugs of tea.

If you don't have snow where you live, seek out some other form of water. Place your hands in the water and take a moment to listen with your hands. This water is connected to all the water on earth, constantly moving, flowing, cleansing. Take some of this water into your body by licking your fingers.

# November 14

Communicating with the natural world requires you to still inner chatter and listen to deeper messages. The Buddhist meditation of witnessing helps you notice that inner chatter so that you can differentiate it from other information. You can sit, walk, or even wash the dishes to practice this mindfulness meditation. Try sitting in a straight-backed chair with your feet flat on the floor. Set a timer for five minutes. As you get more comfortable with the technique, you can lengthen your sit to ten and then twenty minutes. All there is to do is sit and observe your breath moving in and out. When thoughts arise or when you notice yourself thinking, just notice (you might say to yourself, "thinking") and bring your attention back to your breath. The same can be done while walking inside or out. Notice your feet moving on the earth. Bring your attention back when it wanders.

# November 15

Another way to hear your inner voice is to amplify it by using tools of divination. Today, pull out a favorite deck of divination or tarot cards. Before asking any questions of the cards, take a moment to quiet your mind. Attune to the place inside you, maybe somewhere near your heart, where you feel most connected to the Goddess. Breathe with her for a few moments. Know that these cards reflect your connection with the Divine; they are a bridge that helps us put words to the flowing energies of the mystery. You might ask a specific question about a relationship, addiction, dream, or something else, or you might ask for general guidance. Remember, though, that the power of the cards does not lie solely outside of you, nor does it come totally from your human mind. You are a part of the Divine, and the Divine is a part of you.

# November 16

Prayer is communion with the Divine. There are many ways to pray: some look more like asking for guidance, others more like meditation. Walking in the woods is a prayer for me. Chanting is a common form of prayer for Catholics and Buddhists. A prayer of thanks over a meal reminds us that the food on the table is a gift from the Goddess and the earth. Today, before you eat a meal, take a moment to feel the energy of the food on the table. Can you sense its origins? Feel a bit of the road it traveled to come to your table. Does it radiate life force, ready to transform the mantle of the Goddess into another form? Let these sensations and images inspire a prayer. As you eat, consider these bites of food as energy transformed. The earth, sunlight, and water that grew this food from a seed into a plant or plants now transforms into a new form: you. Let eating be a prayer.

# November 17

In Chinese elemental medicine, winter is the season of water, dreams, and the west. Water is a huge issue for our planet today; we have a limited amount of fresh water, which our growing population has a tendency to waste and pollute. Today, practice transmutation, a way to cleanse water. Pour a glass of water or gather some from a stream or a pond. Breathe deeply, entering a meditative state. Attune with the Divine by feeling your heart center. Let that spark of divinity spread into your entire being until you are aware of your own divinity. When you feel a shift in consciousness and unity, focus your attention on your vessel of water. Take a moment to sense its nature. Invite it to reflect its natural divinity, to vibrate at its highest level of being. When you feel a shift in the water, you have transmuted, cleansed, and purified it.

This is a very advanced practice, one to come back to repeatedly. It can transform truly polluted water while changing your relationship with the Divine. For more, see *Medicine for the Earth* by Sandra Ingerman.

# November 18

What grows in your garden this time of year? If you live
in a warmer climate, like gardening zones 9 to 11, you
will have a lovely garden right now. But even if you live
in a colder climate, you may find some cool-season veggies hanging on from last fall even if you do not have a
greenhouse or cold frame (see September 10). Kale, for
instance, is very cold hardy and will often peek defiantly
out of the snow. Some weeds, herbs, and wild plants also
hang in there this time of year. Walk through a garden
or wildland to find a few edible plants, and include them
in tonight's winter salad.

## November 19

Descending into darkness is about entering the depths of our soul's journey. One meditation that represents this journey is walking a labyrinth. A labyrinth is not a maze; you cannot get lost as you walk inward toward the center and then back out to the beginning. You can, however, get disoriented, just as we do during our journeys through life. Walking the labyrinth is a powerful meditation of healing, prayer, reflection, and rejuvenation. Some churches have labyrinths open to the public, or you can make your own by using tape on the floor, a stick in wet sand, stones in the grass, or paint on a patio. This can be as simple as a spiral, or you can find instructions on crafting the traditional labyrinth shape online or in books like those authored by Lauren Artress. The labyrinth connects us with the creative medicine of Spider and the transformative power of Snake. As we walk, we enter the Underworld and return back to the living whole but transformed.

# November 20

Today, do some deep dreamwork. Call up a dream you recently had, one that was meaningful or strange or maybe frightening. Get comfortable, then ground and center. Close your eyes. See yourself reentering this dream. You are your conscious self returning to the dreamscape, not simply remembering what you dreamt. Now ask that a dream guide appear to you. You may have to wait a bit or ask again, but an animal spirit will come to you. Ask it to guide you through the dreamworld. Ask it to help you learn from your dreams. When you are ready, return to normal waking life. Whenever you feel the desire for deep work, return to a dream (one you actually experienced or just let images flow in your deep imagination) and call on your dream guide to help you. You can also call on this dream guide while in ritual space.

# November 21

There are four equally important paths to Spirit, named by theologian Matthew Fox the Via Positiva, Via Negativa, Via Creativa, and Via Transformativa. This time of year we are often drawn to the Via Negativa, where we seek Goddess "in darkness and nothingness, in the silence and emptying, in the letting go and letting be, and in the pain and suffering that constitute an equally real part of our spiritual journey."[5] Sit in stillness today. Notice your desire to fill darkness with light and stillness with movement or thought. Keep returning to the void, trusting, being. Gently draw into your awareness any suffering or pain you've been dealing with recently. Let it sit with you in the stillness. Witness.

# November 22

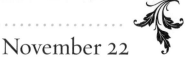

A prayer of gratitude:

I sit in wonder, Goddess (God), at the gift of my body. My breath that moves in and out, an exchange with the world inside me and all around. My heart that pumps blood and oxygen. My brain that processes and thinks and coordinates all I do. My nerves that take in sensation. My feelings that overwhelm and bless.

My body changes over time, but it has been this one body since conception and will be my temple, my avatar, until death. This body dances in the way only it is able to do, carries me from place to place, cries, tastes strawberries, makes love. All I am able to experience in this life is because of this body. Any limitations I face in this life, this body, are both challenges and blessings. For all of this, for my unique body, I give thanks.

# November 23

The sun enters the astrological sign of Sagittarius today. Sagittarians tend to be optimistic, honest, and philosophical. They can become involved in too many projects at once, an easy energy to fall into this time of year. As we celebrate the secular and holy holidays of the season, take time to slow down. Be honest with yourself about your own energy, and focus on the true meanings of the holidays: thankfulness, community, stillness, and family.

Oak is associated with Sagittarius. To realign with the grounded energies of the season rather than the frenetic energy of our culture at this time, go outside, hold an oak leaf in your hand, and face the sun. Breathe. Reconnect with the simple rhythms of autumn folding into winter.

# November 24

In winter we seek out our home, looking for shelter just as animals are in their dens and roots are tucked beneath the earth. For some, this is a time of homecoming, warmth, and connection. For many, though, this is a frustrating and stressful time of year, when the ideal of family clashes with reality. Letting go of what once was, or never was and never will be, is an important part of growing up. It's far from easy, however, especially since our culture doesn't really know how to grow up. Many teen rituals of risk and altered states are actually culturally unsupported attempts to grow up by differentiating from their families and entering the transforming darkness.

Design a ritual of release from your youth, a gateway through which you will step into your soul's purpose. No matter your chronological age, you probably cling to ego aspects of "home." Ritual can be a powerful tool for letting go and moving forward. This might include giving away items and clothes from your past, ritually destroying symbols of your adolescent or young adult personality, grieving, and taking vows to dedicate your "next stage of life to mystery, soul discovery, and the Underworld journey."[6] This ritual will carry into the days and months ahead, depending on how ready you are to move forward. Give yourself time, and trust the path.

# November 25

Today begins the Celtic month of Ruis. The Druid year, named for trees sacred to the ancient Celtic Druids, begins in December, about the time of the winter solstice. It is thirteen moons, or months, long, though in our Gregorian calendar they are tied to fixed dates rather than moons. Each month has the energy and teachings of a tree sacred to the Celts. This month is connected to Ruis, known to us as the elder tree.

As we wind down in both the Celtic and calendar years, consider the energy of Ruis, which is associated with witches, fairies, the Goddess, and protection. Elderberry syrup is one of the best protections against winter colds and will help you heal faster when you do come down with the sniffles. You can make your own by purchasing dried elderberries from a health food or herb shop (or work with a local herbalist to identify them safely in the wild). Simmer a handful of dried berries in a few cups of water on very low heat for about twenty minutes. Strain, compost the berries, and sweeten the syrup with several tablespoons of honey (but do not give honey to infants under one year of age). Store in the refrigerator, and take teaspoonfuls throughout the day to boost your immune system.

# November 26

When we feel stripped of who we once thought we were, we can turn to the earth for guidance and confirmation. Go for a walk today, and look for the first thing that calls to you. It might be a leaf clinging to a branch, a collection of stones, a puddle. Whether you live in a city, near a beach, by a forest, or in the desert, nature will talk to you if you open up and listen. It will help guide you along the path of mystery. Sit with the thing that has attracted you and let whatever happens arise. Imagine you are dreaming with nature. What dreams come?

If it's too cold or miserable to go outside, save your walk for another day, but take some time for yourself to look out the window. Nature speaks in many ways, so you might even find guidance within the walls of your house: a houseplant, a pet, even the steam rolling off a cup of tea. Let yourself dream with the mystery.

# November 27

Sometimes we feel productive, extroverted, and full of energy. Ideas come quickly and easily, and you know exactly how to apply them to life.

And sometimes we *don't* feel that way.

A capitalist society values economic value—and therefore activity devoid of any other influence—over everything else. It's easy to forget that active and productive aren't the only ways to be. As we cycle with the seasons, the moon, weather, daylight, and body metabolism, we will move in and out of fast and slow, light and dark. Notice your highs and lows, and honor them in whatever way you can.

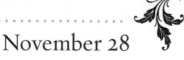

# November 28

*"My blood is holy nourishment. My blood
nourishes the growing fetus. My blood becomes
milk to nourish the young child. My blood
flows into the ground as holy nourishment for
the Great Mother, Gaia, Mother Earth."*

Susun Weed[7]

Give back something to the mother that nourishes us
by pouring some of your moonblood or urine on the
earth. Urine diluted 20:1 with water makes a high nitrogen fertilizer (that I swear repels squirrels), and blood
is high in iron and nitrogen (and also repels squirrels!).
The blood from the giblet bag in your Thanksgiving
turkey can also be poured on the earth, ritually giving
back in thanks for the gift of the bird's life. If you don't
bleed, eat vegetarian, and it's too cold to pee outside,
get in the habit of putting your nail clippings and hair
from your hairbrush in the compost pile. Return what
you can to the land.

# November 29

Continuing with the moonblood theme, it's time to switch to reusable menstrual care if you haven't already. Don't let the pad and tampon industry take all your money just to produce plastic waste. Cloth pads last a long time and are easy to use and easy to wash. GladRags and Lunapads make cute, comfy pads and panty liners (see gladrags.com/faq.htme and lunapads.com/media/image/media-articles/a planet friendly period.pdf). With a yard or so of flannel, some snaps, and a serger sewing machine, you can easily make your own.

Or, if pads aren't your thing, get yourself a reusable menstrual cup that collects your blood (which you can then pour on your garden or into the outdoor compost).

Having both options is nice—you'll never buy the trashy kind again.

# November 30

A simple ritual that can be done every day but which is especially helpful this time of year is to visualize your roots growing deep into the earth. Take several centering breaths and feel your feet or sit bones on the ground. Bring your attention to the energy inside your body—the vibration and awareness pulsing inside. As you breathe, see this energy grow stronger. Let it melt down your legs and into the earth, deep, deeper. Breathe with the crystalline core of the earth as long as possible. This might take two minutes as you stand in line at the grocery store (no one will know!) or a full hour in ritual.

# December 1

Eating in season attunes us with the rhythms of the land and usually means a lighter carbon footprint. Make a salad of winter plants, either from your cold frame (see September 10), the supermarket, or a farmers' market. Root vegetables like beets, fingerling potatoes, and carrots are delicious roasted, then cubed (let them cool a bit before cubing), left warm or cooled, and put on top of a salad. For greens, try spinach, kale, mizuna, or whatever hearty dark greens look vibrant and enticing. Top with some roasted pumpkin seeds or sunflower seeds saved from the end of summer. A simple dressing of balsamic vinegar, olive oil, salt, pepper, and garlic complete the wintery feast.

# December 2

*Sacred space is within us. Not in our body or brain cells but in the volume of our consciousness. Wherever we go, we bring the sacred within us to the sacred around us.*

· · · · · ·

Michael S. Schneider[8]

What if grocery stores, the place most of us get our nourishment, were regarded as sacred? What if we treated our cars as sacred chariots? What if schools were temples of sacred learning? I don't mean religious, I mean sacred, which often gets confused but which transcends all cultures and spiritual paths. Where do you spend most of your time? Make it more sacred by bringing attention, awareness, and gratitude into that space. First bring attention to the "volume of our consciousness" and into that sacred space within. Then let it expand into your external space—your desk, kitchen, car, anywhere you spend time and energy. How does it change your awareness? Plants, stones, and other natural items can also help us create sacred space. Remember, however, that it is your inner power inviting the stone or plant to express its own divinity that makes it sacred to you.

# December 3

Masaru Emoto writes that "every time we look deep into the power of water, we end up affirming the existence of the Divine."[9] In his books about his research into water, Emoto illustrates the power of water to absorb and transmit energy, be it love and gratitude (which Emoto sees as water's basic message) or hate and pollution. He shows this power through photographs of frozen water crystals that have been exposed to words and prayers.

Find some snow or ice, and take a moment to send it love and gratitude. Send to it your intention that it will become clean and free of any pollution it picked up as it journeyed along the water cycle. As it melts or evaporates, it will send this cleansed and heightened energy into the world.

# December 4

Start some indoor potted herb seeds today. Many garden centers will have a rack of seeds tucked out of the way, awaiting spring. Parsley, basil, chives, cilantro, and even lettuces can be grown in pots in a bright but not too hot window. Keep them evenly moist; covering the pot with plastic (reuse those plastic bag packing pillows by cutting them open or use a clean produce bag) will help retain moisture until the seeds germinate. While generally I am a fan of accepting where the seasons are right now, a little splash of spring can brighten the day, encourage cooking at home, and help us feel connected to green and growing things.

# December 5

Early December is the time to put up the Yule tree. It's my favorite holiday tradition, an altar to evergreen trees, a light in the darkness, and it encompasses my Germanic and Scandinavian ancestral traditions. It is both Pagan and Christian. The tree is a work of art, a gathering place, and a symbol of life in the midst of the otherwise dormant earth.

Purchase a locally grown, pesticide-free tree by searching for local growers or sustainably harvested US Forest Service trees. Never get your tree flocked; the chemicals are toxic. A live tree is another option, though it cannot be kept indoors as long and should be brought inside close to Yule, then brought outside promptly to a protected area to await spring planting. In climates where evergreens do not grow naturally, consider making a different plant, like a houseplant or even a cactus, your Yule tree. If you opt for a "fake" tree, con-

secrate it each year by smudging it with smoke (fire and air) and sprinkling a little water and salt (earth) onto its branches.

Let the raising and decorating of your tree be a ritual honoring life and light. Invite fairies to live in its branches, asking that they, in turn, protect your home.

# December 6

Every year we make a few tree ornaments. An easy and very adaptable way to make ornaments is to make salt dough. The simple recipe makes a dough both kids and adults can craft with.

Mix 2 cups white (wheat) flour with 1 cup salt and add 1 cup water, kneading until smooth. Using your hands, clay-shaping tools, or cookie cutters, shape the dough into desired shapes. The ornaments shouldn't be thicker than about ¾ inch anywhere or they will take too long to dry out. Bake until hard, about 1½ hours, in a 325°F oven, then paint using acrylic paints or glitter glue.

Symbols of Yule include the usual mainstream Christmas symbols of trees, snowflakes, and stars as well as the sun, fairies, gnomes, and the Holly King. Consider that the ornaments are made out of earth (salt and wheat), water, fire (the oven), and air (your inspirations).

# December 7

Because of the way water molecules bond, frozen water elicits some unique properties that other liquids do not. One of them is that water expands, or gets less dense, at 4°C, or just above its freezing point. When it freezes, it has a very low density. This results in several outcomes that make life on earth possible.

Large bodies of water freeze from the top down (because low-density ice floats), allowing for plants and animals to live under the frozen ice even in very cold areas like the planet's poles. Surface ice also reflects sunlight back into space, helping to cool the planet. "The large heat capacity of the oceans and seas allows them to act as heat reservoirs such that sea temperatures vary only a third as much as land temperatures and so moderate our climate (for example, the Gulf Stream carries tropical warmth to northwestern Europe)," writes Martin Chaplin in his essay "Anomalous Properties of

Water."[10] Whether you drop ice into a cool drink or go skating on a lake, send water molecules thanks for their unique properties that allow our planet to be a home to intelligent and complex life.

# December 8

Water fills the stems and roots of plants. It helps stabilize hemoglobin. Its hydrostatic nature, pulling against gravity, determines the maximum height of trees. Even the center of living bone contains 75 percent water. As you read yesterday, water stabilizes the planet. It is the structure of all life. It is our life-support system. Water is support.

Pour yourself a glass of water. Visualize the water running from melted snow down the mountains and into reservoirs, lakes, and streams, then through pipes to your home. See it fill the glass, noticing its nature to rise up the side of the glass and to fill the space it enters. Drink. Let it fill your inner space. Let it support you.

# December 9

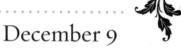

Water epitomizes support and also grace—in both meanings of the word. Picture an arching wave and a spilling cascade of water. Dancers seek such grace and flow. Another meaning of the word *grace* is "a virtue coming from God" (*Merriam-Webster*). Virtue is usually thought of as a human trait, but it comes from the ideas of strength and excellence. Water certainly possesses both.

Sit with a bowl of water or snow. Ground and center. Enter the essence of the water in your lap by reaching your awareness into the substance. Sit with this gift of strength and grace.

# December 10

> *Grace is a mystical substance, not a mental concept. As a mystical substance, it must be experienced....To know grace fully and directly, you must turn inward.*

Caroline Myss[11]

Grace is usually presented in a Christian context, but it is a "substance" or gift that defies religion. Grace is that moment of touching the Divine. It is when the light enters and frees or heals us. It is a blessing. I believe the feeling we seek this time of year, whatever our religious leanings, is a sense of grace. We celebrate the return of the light as candles lit over several days, as the birth of a savior/teacher, and as the rebirth of the sun. That moment, that breath of life—that is grace. Meditate on the sense of grace in your life or write about it in your journal. How have you felt this kiss of eternal love?

## December 11

*"Caring for the earth and caring for the soul are interrelated."*
. . . . . .
Satish Kumar[12]

Meditate on the above quote, then write a poem or paint a picture about the interrelation of soil and soul.

How does this meditation on their relationship inspire you toward caring for both—and for yourself? What insights about matter and spirit arise? How can you bring these ideas into daily life?

# December 12

Satish Kumar has said that every movement needs a trinity of words to explain and direct it, like "reduce, reuse, recycle" and "life, liberty, and the pursuit of happiness." He suggests "soil, soul, and society" as the inspiration for the awakened ecological era. Yesterday we explored the relationship between soil and soul. Both soil and soul are sacred, and when we care for both, we are led to care for ourselves and others. This is the movement that Kumar wishes to encourage by naming our trinity Soil, Soul, and Society: when we build a culture on holding these three as sacred, we can heal our relationships with each other and the earth. Earth, Spirit, and Community are all crucial aspects of whole living.

This holiday season, pick an issue affecting society—hunger, poverty, education, etc.—and donate whatever sum you can afford to healing this cause or spend some time volunteering. Educate your children, if you have them, about this cause and why you want to help.

# December 13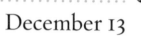

In what other ways can you become actively involved in Soil, Soul, and Society? What physical action can you personally take? Choose a small thing to which you are drawn and come up with a plan for action. Again, if you have them, involve your children. You might donate produce you grew to a homeless shelter, or collect books to send to an orphanage in Africa (see http://kabiza.com /send-a-book-child-in-africa.htm or http://shareafrica .org/donate/send-books-toys-shoes-clothes or http:// www.booksforafrica.org/index.html), or get involved in revitalizing your neighborhood school. What is calling you? How can you get involved?

# December 14

One way to unite Soil, Soul, and Society is through community gardens, community supported agriculture (CSA), or simply sharing your gardening with your neighbors. While the garden rests (for most climates in the Northern Hemisphere), lay the groundwork for this sort of community-based gardening. You might look up a local CSA and purchase a share, sign up to join a community garden (a great place to learn how to garden if you are a newbie), or plan an edible front yard that will attract neighbors. You can teach others about growing your own food while beautifying your home. Visit the American Community Garden Association website at communitygarden.org. To find a CSA in your area, visit www.localharvest.org/csa. And for ideas on growing edibles in your front yard, check out *The Edible Front Yard* by Ivette Soler and *Edible Landscaping* by Rosalind Creasy.

# December 15

Go outside. Sit. Listen. Often we spend too much time indoors this time of year, surrounded by holiday lights and incessant holiday tunes. While these traditions can be cozy, they can also overwhelm the nervous system. Sit in the stillness of the coming winter. Journal about what you see, hear, smell, and feel while simply sitting outside.

# December 16

Make your own incense. You probably have many ingredients available outside your front door: juniper boughs and berries, a small piece of cedar, some dried needles from the Yule tree, or some winter-dried herbs like rosemary or sage. In the kitchen you will find dried orange peel, cinnamon, and cloves. Rub wood or bark (cinnamon, for instance) on sandpaper to make a fine powder. Grind up dried plant matter and spices in a mortar and pestle. Begin with a tablespoon of rough herbs (like dried berries) and a teaspoon of powdered ingredients, adjusting amounts to your smell preferences. Blend well, adding a few drops of frankincense or myrrh essential oil (optional). Burn in a heat-proof container on charcoal blocks (available where incense is sold) or toss into the hearth fire to burn.

# December 17

Traditionally in northern cultures winter was a time to gather around the fire, tell stories, and rest. We ate root vegetables, which are grounding and nourishing, and made meals from the foods we had canned and salted last autumn. We mended clothes and linens, whittled wooden toys, and listened to the wind howling down the chimney. Give yourself a day to set aside the holiday to-do list. Light a fire or a candle and do a craft, play a game, or write a letter to a friend using a pen and paper. Feel how the rhythm of the earth at this time is about going inward and nourishing yin energy. Let yourself attune with this rhythm.

## December 18

Reflect on the last six and a half weeks since Samhain. In your journal, write out any words that come to mind when you think back on your journey, either through this devotional or other spiritual work you've been doing. You have faced death and entered the healing power of the womb. You've listened to your dreams and inner voice. You have meditated on the miracle of water. How has this work changed you? What questions linger? What fears remain?

# December 19

Take three of the words you wrote yesterday that feel inspirational. Gather three small objects to represent them, something you can carry in a pocket like small stones, beads, or acorns. Sit before a lit candle with your three little tokens before you. Say each word, sending it into an object. Feel the object become infused with the energy of this inspirational word. Ground yourself, then snuff the candle when you are finished. Now carry the three objects with you as you go through your holiday celebrations. They can be kept private or shared, but the important thing is to take them with you as reminders of the sacred path you walk.

## December 20

In the days and hours leading up to the birth of my children, I wanted dark and quiet. With my first child I craved the low tones of Tibetan chanting and the didgeridoo. I felt heavy, dark, and ripe—and uncomfortable.

Can you feel the deep tones of the earth, ready for the rebirth of the sun? How does it relate to your own sense of excitement or anxiety? Watch the sun set if you can. Notice your emotions—the bittersweet longing, the sadness, the release. Breathe.

# Yule

Yule, the winter solstice, marks the shortest day of light and the longest night. After this night, the sun will rise just a little bit earlier and set just a little bit later. The coldest time of the year, however, is yet to come in many places. Yule is a time of contrasts—ice and chill and brittleness balanced by the warmth of indoor lights, fires, the hearth, and community. It is the darkest time of year, but it carries the promise of light. All holidays celebrated at this time of year relate to this idea that there is light and hope even in the deepest darkness. Carry that message with you, as it is true for your own life and spiritual journey as well.

# December 21

On this longest night of the year, spend some time getting to know the darkness. Turn off all the lights, electric and otherwise. You might even want to turn off the power to your house at the circuit breaker, if possible. We are inundated by electromagnetic frequencies twenty-four hours a day. While it is no longer possible to completely avoid EMFs anywhere in a "developed" country, you can turn off as much as possible and sit in the silence. Mainstream culture tends to fear darkness and stillness. We fill it with holiday lights, cell phones, computers, and general noise. But darkness can be healing, like a return to the womb. When we are stripped of all distractions, we can find the Goddess in the stillness, where there is nothing but your soul and the Divine. Sit in this space, being cleansed, being healed.

After a while, light one candle. Notice how you feel as the light returns.

# December 22

Today the sun enters Capricorn, the humorous if some-times grumpy sign of the goat. Capricorns are tradition-ally practical, ambitious, and patient. They can be overly rigid. Self-confidence is an issue with many Capricorns: they can be overly confident or suffer from pessimism, low self-confidence, and a feigned laziness. They also have a tendency to worry. What is worrying you now, eating away at your self-confidence? Write it out, then go bury the paper in the earth—Capricorn is an earth sign, and turning to the grounding, healing power of the earth can help us all release worry and poor self-esteem. If the ground is too frozen, bury your paper under a rock, and let the structure of the earth provide you with support.

# December 23

Today is known as Ailm, or silver fir, in the Celtic tree months. It is a day out of time. In a lunar calendar, there are thirteen months, each twenty-eight days long. That adds up to 364 days. Since a year is usually 365 days long, there is designated a day out of time. In some sources, this day is not named for any tree. In others, today is named for Ailm.

This tree is dedicated to the Birth Mother Goddess.[13] Interestingly, mainstream Christian culture is about to celebrate another famous birth mother. Many new Pagans struggle with whether or not to celebrate Christmas or Yule—are they selling out if they celebrate the holiday of their youth? Are they rejecting all their childhood memories of secular or religious Christmases if they celebrate Yule? These two holidays, as well as other December holidays celebrating light, are about the rebirth of light in the world. Why not draw on symbols and traditions from both holidays? On your altar or Yule/Christmas tree, include both; Mary and the Mother Goddess are both welcome, as are the newborn babe, the Sun, and symbols from other winter holidays.

# December 24

The Druid month of Beith, or birch, begins today. Birch represents cleansing and purification.[14] Take a ritual bath or shower today. Before stepping into the water, light a candle or some incense (make sure it's in a safe place), and take a moment to ground and center. State aloud or in your mind what you wish to release or purify. Dedicate this bath or shower to that purpose. While bathing, see the energy you wish to cleanse seeping out of your pores and into the purifying water. As you drain the tub or leave the shower, thank the earth for purifying and recycling what you no longer need.

If you have access to a birch tree (or even some birch wood, like a wand), spend some time with it today, feeling your purified self ready to move forward into the coming year.

# December 25

The smell of oranges always reminds me of Christmas. Oranges and other citrus fruits, as well as persimmons and pomegranates, ripen in the southern continents' summer, which is the northern continents' winter. One of the double-edged swords of our modern culture is that we can ship foods from thousands of miles away. While this burns large amounts of fossil fuels, it also means our cornucopia is always full with a wide variety of fruits and vegetables from around the planet. (Can you imagine the ecological impact if we were to convert all the trucks that transport food to renewable fuel sources?)

Nuts and fall-ripened fruits like pears, apples, and cranberries are also featured at this time of year, and if you live in the Northern Hemisphere, they probably carry a smaller carbon footprint. The Christmas fruit bowl includes some of these fruits as well. Interestingly,

these two groups of foods—those shipped from the south and those grown in northern climates—often go well together, like oranges with cranberries. They are often both featured in the cornucopia, or (cow's) horn of plenty, an ancient Roman symbol of the Goddess.

As you gather with family today, include in your prayers or discussions acknowledgment of the coming together of the planet's foods. What other foods are traditional in your family? For these gifts we are truly blessed.

## December 26

Journal topic:

Yule is about the return of the sun, Christmas honors the birth of the son, and at this time other religions celebrate light in the midst of darkness. Darkness can be like emptiness and despair or it can be like the cozy warmth of a quilt. The dark can mean facing demons or preparing for birth. What form of darkness has been present for you lately? Can you feel rays of light shining upon these darkened corners? What images of darkness and light have been appearing in your dreams and waking life?

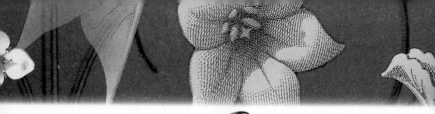

## December 27

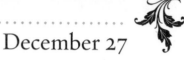

> *I could not chatter away as I used to do, taking it all for granted. My words now must be as slow, as new, as single, as tentative, as the steps I took going down the path away from the house, between the dark-branched, tall dancers motionless against the winter shining.*

Ursula K. Le Guin, "She Unnames Them"[15]

The light was reborn at the winter solstice, and the days are already longer. Let yourself be reborn. Go outside and see the world as if for the first time. Let the names of things and your associations with them fall away. Notice how light hits the land. If you have snow or ice available, examine it close-up. Stare at those fluffy white things over you—imagine never having seen clouds; you don't even know what those things are called. Look and look again at the world, and let the world show you who she is.

## December 28

Post-holiday disappointment or depression is not uncommon. If your family stirred up your issues or if financial stresses got in the way of joy or if you associate this time of year with difficult times, you might encounter melancholy and insecurity. Or perhaps you love the holidays, but they never seem to quite reach that fantasy in your mind—and here you are, another year passed.

One thing that always helps me when I'm in such a funk is to spend time in nature. On a warm winter day I'll go see what's growing in the garden or walk in a brown and icy park. Just taking a cup of tea out to the patio to breathe cool air and watch the trees laced against the sky helps me reconnect with peace and let go of expectation and bustle. Nature helps us let go and just be.

# December 29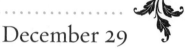

One of the beauties of honoring the Wheel of the Year is that we celebrate the sabbats as they roll along, not just as points along the path. After a sabbat we are fully in the energy of that holy time, rather than past a holiday. Instead of having to clean up the mess and move on, each day we can settle into the energy and teaching of a solar and earth phase. The days after a sabbat are just as much that holiday as the days leading up to it.

Sit before a few lit candles. White is nice, but any candle color will do. Ground, center, and let your energy radiate outwards into the day or night. Feel the pulse of the land. Can you feel the subtle return of the light? It is growing. The sun rises ever so slightly farther north. The chill deepens. Let images and senses fall over you as you feel the energy of the days just past Yule.

## December 30

An herbal face steam can recharge and renew in any season. It can be part of a skin-care regimen and personal spa routine or practiced on its own. A face steam is also great for clearing the sinuses. The steam opens pores and aligns us with the healing powers of water, fire, earth, and air.

Bring four cups of filtered water to a boil, and put small handfuls of bulk herbs into a large stainless-steel or glass bowl. Good choices for this time of year are dried rose petals, sage, rosemary, and lavender. Add no more than a single drop of any essential oil, for they are potent. Pour the boiling water over the herbs. Cover your head with a clean towel that is large enough to cover your head and drape over the bowl of steam. Sit for ten minutes over the bowl, breathing in the healing scents of herbs and steam.

# December 31

Perform a smudge on yourself, your home, and your belongings today. Smudging is burning an herb and using the smoke to cleanse, aligning yourself and your environment with the chosen plant's vision of wellness. Each plant has its own sacred truth. When you work with a plant by ingesting it, smudging with it, or including it in your garden, you connect with its sacred truth. This truth might be strength, integrity, clarity, support, or any number of other sacred energies.

In smudging, writes Loren Cruden in *Medicine Grove,* "the subtle, pervasive nature of smoke, the transformative presence of fire, and the evocative medicine of the plant's fragrance release the herb's essential message into deep levels of consciousness."[16] A common smudging herb is white sage, which carries the medicine of purification. Another is *Artemisia ludoviciana,* also known as prairie sage, which aligns us with the dispersal of negativity and the protection of sacred space.

To smudge, light a dried herb bundle and waft the smoke with your hand or a feather over your body, doorways, objects, and areas. Ground and center yourself, and move prayerfully through your home as you cleanse it with the smoke. Set an intention for the calendar year ahead that is aligned with the medicine of your chosen plant.

# January 1

The name of this month comes from the Roman god Janus, who looks forward and back. He teaches of past wisdom and future knowledge. He guards doorways and thresholds as well as harbors and the seasons. Janus is also a god of communication.

This is a crucial time to call on Janus as we marry past wisdom and future knowledge—ancient ways and new technologies—in order to face climate change. Do a meditation or ritual calling on Janus's wisdom. See a doorway in front of you, and step up to the threshold. Feel your feet firmly on the ground and your crown energy connected to the universe. Hold one palm facing up and the other down, like a whirling dervish. Call on Janus. Ask him to guide our species forward so we are able to communicate respectfully with each other through these challenging times. Picture ancient wisdom, such as Hopi dryland farming, and modern technology, such as solar panels. See these pictures in your hands, and bring them together by pressing your palms together. Ask Janus to bless this transition time and help us to find success as a people, as a planet. Gather energy in yourself fueled by your love for the earth and all people. Direct that energy into the earth.

# January 2

Climate scientists have determined that we must put no more than 350 parts per million of carbon dioxide into the atmosphere in order for the planet to be moderately livable for humans and most other plants and animals that have likewise evolved during the last 10,000 years. Currently there is about 390 ppm.[17]

One organization working to pressure policy makers into changing this is 350.org. Take a little time today to check out their website and find a way to get involved. There are local chapters and groups all over the world. Activism projects range from public art to online international protest projects to physical marches. They offer workshops and community support. You can get very involved or just sign a few petitions. Every bit makes a difference.

# January 3

The Findhorn garden and community in northern Scotland is famous for growing forty-pound cabbages and roses that bloom in the snow. The founders of Findhorn, Eileen and Peter Caddy and Dorothy Maclean, moved to a trailer park in northern Scotland on guidance Eileen received in meditation. Their ability to grow miraculous gardens came from these communications as well as Maclean's communication with the devas, or nature spirits.[18]

The ability to open and trust such guidance comes from practice. Today, sit in a quiet space and send your attention into the land you care for—your garden, back patio, neighborhood, or city. Offer the intention that you be given guidance for making the land a balanced and vibrant home for humans, plants, and animals. Sit, breathe, and listen. You may receive communication via words, images, felt senses, or a combination of these. It

may be one small thing or a flood of information. Allow it to come. Don't worry about validating the information just yet. When you are finished, ground and center. Record your experience in your journal, then act on what you are able to.

# January 4

Not everyone receives snow, but if and when you do, try to take a night walk during that magical time when the snow stops, and all is still and bright. You will not need a flashlight, especially if the moon is out. There is a special camaraderie with your walking mates. Children and adults alike discover a fairyland of magical crystals and snow glow. And the quiet—there is nothing like it in our busy world.

# January 5

The beautiful children's book *Owl Moon* by Jane Yolen chronicles a young girl's rite of passage looking for owls with her father on a moonlit, snowy night. This is a good time of year to look for owls in the continental US, for they migrate ever so slightly south at this time (though you can see some species year-round). Many owls are nocturnal, but some, like the great gray owl, are diurnal, hunting at dawn and dusk.

Owl teaches us about illumination, clairvoyance, and magic, and is associated with wisdom, for Owl can "see that which others cannot."[19] Owl also heralds initiation,[20] a transition from one thing to another, as twilight transitions us from day to night. If you see or hear an owl, pay attention to transitions in your life. What needs illuminating? Let Owl be your guide as you tap intuitively into the great pattern to gain wisdom about your life situation.

# January 6

Set up a simple weather station to help you attune to the signs of shifts in the weather. Through regularly observing your data and comparing it to what you observe, you will develop a keen weather sense. You will begin to notice the exact shade of the sky on a night that will snow, the direction of the wind that spells rain, and the stillness that comes before a storm. You may begin to sense long-term forecasts, too, such as rain a few days out, just by listening to the shifts in the weather. A weather station can help attune you to these signs. Include a thermometer, rain gauge, barometer, and weather vane. You can buy these from garden centers and science gift or toy stores, or you can make your own. See http://www.salemclock.com/weather/weather01 .htm or inquire at your local science museum about possible workshops.

# January 7

When you take down your Yule tree, do not just throw it in the trash. Many municipalities offer free tree mulching services, with lovely evergreen mulch for the taking. You might also stick the undecorated tree into a snow bank and decorate with pine cone birdseed treats (push nut butter into a pine cone and roll it in birdseed). Or cut up your tree and save the branches to ritually burn next Yule. Use the branches as mulch over perennials. A chunk of the trunk makes the perfect Yule log.

# January 8

The Danish Snow Queen, Japanese Yuki Onna, and German Holda are all fairies or goddesses of winter, ice, and snow. They represent the extreme beauty of winter and its fierce danger. They carry with them the wisdom of reflection, as in a silver shard of ice. Holda, also known as Hel in Nordic realms, is associated with the crone aspect of the moon. Holda and Hel are also associated with dark magic and revenge.[21]

Feelings of revenge and the desire to harm others call not for violent action but for serious self-reflection. What is it that we are reacting to? How can we find healing in this situation? Can we emulate the Snow Queen and freeze the moment for a while, look into our own darkness, and find healing? Spring will come eventually, and the situation will thaw. If you face a trying situation, call on the transformational wisdom of winter to help you through.

## January 9

If you can find a large body of ice such as a frozen reservoir or a lake, go listen to it. It needs to be frozen several inches deep. Ice this big makes the most wonderful noises—creaking and popping, groaning and whistling. It reminds me of humpback whales…or maybe alien communication. The sound comes from air trapped beneath the ice, as well as from the ice itself. It is the voice of the ice, of the land, of winter.

# January 10

Gather a cupful of snow and set it in a warm place to melt. Notice how little water you get and how much dirt is in it. Despite the dirt, my children love to eat snow and to suck on icicles; I figure a little dirt won't kill them. Tasting "wild" snow and ice shocks your body into really experiencing the intensity of winter. Indulge your inner child and let a few snowflakes or ice crystals melt on your tongue. If you live in a climate without ice and snow, find a river made of snow melt. Dip your finger in and taste it. Feel the river or the snow, and feel the bigger connection of the water cycle, the mountains, the clouds, and the cold temperatures that come from being tilted away from the sun.

# January 11

Every snowflake has six sides. Bee's hives are made of hexagons, too, as are the spaces in bones. Six is a strong number; the hexagon perfectly balances weight on all sides. In esoterica, a hexagram is seen as the female yoni, the downward triangle, and the male lingam, the upward-pointing triangle, imposed on each other. In the Jewish Kabala, six is associated with beauty, harmony, and majesty, certainly feelings that are evoked when looking at magnified snowflakes or a bees' hive. Look for sixes today—in shapes and in numerals—and pause for a moment to allow yourself to settle into beauty and harmony.

# January 12

Another weather pattern I associate with January (in addition to snow, which of course doesn't fall everywhere) is crystalline blue sky and temperatures of just above zero. I am reminded of the Japanese sun goddess Amaterasu. When her brother killed one of her attendants, Amaterasu retreated into a cave, plunging the world into darkness. The Japanese gods and goddesses, desperate for the sun, set a rooster outside her cave, along with a magical mirror or jewel. When the rooster crowed, she wondered how it could be morning without her and peeked out of the cave. She was greeted by the brilliance of her own light reflected in the mirror. She then understood the power of her own light and promised never to hide it again.

Let the bright chill of January be a great mirror. Look into Amaterasu's mirror to see your shining self reflected. Journal about your own light. Where do you see it shining or reflected in others? In what ways do you share your light?

YULE

# January 13

If it gets cold enough where you live, go in search of ice art. Ice freezes in lovely fractals on single-pane windows. In mud it makes hoar frost towers that remind me of Superman's snow palace. It can cause dangerous but stunning displays of frozen branches and entire trees coated in ice. Icicles, white and cracked lakes, and clear, bubbly ice on the water trough all display ice art. Perhaps you live where lakes push sheets of ice up onto shore, or you may only see ice as frosted dew at the edges of grass in the early morning. What kinds of ice art can you find? Take your camera with you as you search for the beauty in the ice.

## January 14

When—and if—it does snow, pile it up around trees and hedges, especially if you live where daytime temperatures can melt the snow quickly, exposing tree trunks to sun scald and freezing wind. The snow provides insulation. As it melts, it irrigates the tree. Filling cisterns and buckets with snow that can be used to water the spring garden is another way to utilize snow for irrigation. For thousands of years, dryland farmers have collected snow for use later when there is no precipitation.

# January 15

The Sami, or Native people of northern Scandinavia and Russia, believe that every place has a spirit. Does your land have a different spirit, or feel to it, in winter? As a self-guided meditation or by writing a story, imagine you are walking on the land near you—in your yard, neighborhood, forest, or field—and you come upon the spirit of the land. It is winter. Greet the spirit respectfully, and ask it to communicate with you. What does it look like? How does it feel? What does it tell you about itself?

You might also sit outside and try to feel the energy or spirit of the place, then ask the spirit to reveal itself to you in your dreams.

# January 16

Take at least one cold day to visit a local arboretum or botanical garden. The steamy tropical house is an antidote to the long, cold month of January, while walking outside in cold weather offers a new glimpse of the gardens you do not get in summer. I brought my two-year-old, all bundled up, to the Denver Botanic Gardens one January day when the high was only sixteen degrees Fahrenheit. We had the gardens completely to ourselves. The shrubs, trees, and arbors draped and tucked beneath thick snow showed me a whole other personality of the gardens. I could see the coming spring beneath the snow while being completely immersed in the beauty of winter.

# January 17

Cold weather is a time for hot cereal in the mornings. Year-round farmers' markets or local-only markets will be able to tell you what grains are grown locally. Try a local grain with local dried fruits and some local honey. Hardier grains like whole oats, wheat berries, or wild rice can be put in the slow cooker the night before, then served hot first thing in the morning (add a little more water than the usual ratio). Top with local cream or your favorite dairy substitute. If local grains are hard to come by or if those grown in or near your state don't fit your dietary needs, try some heirloom and lesser-known grains or seeds like red quinoa or amaranth.

# January 18

To save energy in winter, try a few of the following ideas:

- Turn on your oven once and use it efficiently by roasting and baking a bunch of meals one night a week—throw in squash, beets, a pie, a chicken, some potatoes ... then reheat quickly in a pan later in the week or eat cold as a salad.

- Set your thermostat lower at night and during the day to keep the furnace from kicking on so much. Blankets and sweaters are cozy!

- Invest in some insulating window coverings.

- Get an energy audit, available from your local electricity company and many solar power companies, to identify heat leaks.

- Eat by candlelight.

- Hang laundry outside early, giving it time to dry in the cooler days.

# January 19

Set one night a week that is "gadget free": no computers, TV, or phones. Play old-fashioned board games, word games, or charades. Tell stories. Knit—or learn how. Have a talent show. Or just read together, aloud or to yourselves. If you have children, this will not only teach them how to entertain themselves without gadgets, it will help them feel the rhythms of *kairos*—unstructured "now" time, living in the present, eternal moment. It will reconnect the whole family, regardless of age. If you don't have children, it will do the same for you, helping you to slow down and rely on old-fashioned modes of entertainment. Consider hosting a gadget-free event for friends, too, especially those with young people.

# January 20

Winter is a good time to spot raptors like eagles and hawks, as they are not hidden by foliage and may have to come out in the open to look for winter-scarce food. Visit fields or rivers lined with trees, where raptors hunt, and bring binoculars. "Eagle medicine is the power of the Great Spirit, the connection to the Divine. It is the ability to live in the realm of spirit and yet remain connected and balanced within the realm of earth," write Sams and Carson in *The Medicine Cards*.[22] Ecospiritual paths can draw on Eagle medicine. When faced with the degradation of the sacred earth, it's easy to get angry and righteous. It's easy also to get ungrounded when we follow a spiritual path. Eagles fly, but they are far from ungrounded. They remain connected to both worlds and use their keen skills of observation and vision to get right to the point.

# January 21

The sun enters Aquarius today. Aquarians tend to be independent and private but also friendly, with a genuine desire to serve others. They have an original, idealistic streak and are drawn to the arts, sciences, and social service fields. Aquarians are curious, but their opinions on things can become ossified. The environmental movement relies on Aquarian traits of curiosity and innovation, service and idealism. If you could invent something that would solve our energy needs, clean up pollution, or help endangered animals, what would it be? Draw or write in your journal about this ideal innovation. Let yourself play. Then let yourself be curious—does something like this exist? Should it?

# January 22

The Celtic month of Luis began on January 21. The Welsh name for Luis is *Cerdinen*, named for the Druid sacred tree of rowan. The energy of Luis is learning and quickening.[23] We are always learning and growing. Often an idea slumbers inside for some time; we begin to feel its presence at the time of quickening, just as a pregnant woman feels the first sweet movements of her babe. What is beginning to make itself known to you? What is it calling you to learn? Write a list today of what you want to learn or pursue in the coming months. As the light lengthens and the world begins to thaw, let your inner calling follow these projects and ideas.

# January 23

In many places, this is the time to buy winter clothes as stores mark them down to make room for spring items. Consider as you shop that it takes about a bathtub full of water to make a cotton T-shirt and a considerable amount of fossil fuel as well. Shopping at used clothing stores not only saves you money, it reduces your carbon and water footprint by a lot. Treat yourself to a thrift store run today.

While you are combing the winter sales (thrift stores have them too!), consider snagging a few extra coats and blankets in good condition to donate to shelters. Also go through your own closets—what coats and blankets do you no longer wear but are still in good condition? Many climates still face a lot of cold days ahead, and people in need still need warm winter clothing, sleeping bags, and blankets. Often the holiday clothing and blanket drives have been exhausted. If you don't see notices of local drives for warm clothes and blankets, call the local shelters to see how you can help.

# January 25

Step outside to see your breath puff white clouds. As you breathe in, your air passages warm the chill, keeping your internal temperature fairly constant. While you exchange oxygen and carbon dioxide, you also exchange heat with the world outside your skin. The outside changes you a little, and you change the outside: you can see that change, this little cloud of your breath. Become aware of the island of life that is your body. Inside your skin buzz myriad processes that make up this thing we call being alive. Outside swirls air, water, pollutants, smells, the exhalations of trees and birds and the family dog. Pause for a moment. Breathe. Feel the patient, persistent miracle of being alive.

# January 26

A variety of birds can be attracted to your yard year-round. In January, birds will appreciate a high-calorie seed mix with lots of black-oil sunflower seeds, as well as suet and peanuts. You will attract chickadees, nuthatches, jays, and woodpeckers. In the Midwest, cardinals will flock to your sunflower seed feeders. You can also see juncos and pine siskins in most parts of the US in winter; they migrate to Alaska and Canada for the warmer months. Juncos like white millet scattered on the ground, while pine siskins will be drawn to nyjer (also called black thistle) seed, which needs a special feeder.[24]

# January 27

Panentheism addresses the idea that God is found both outside of us—a transcendent god—but also within. God is in us, and we are in God. We find the Goddess by looking deeply into her creation: the earth and our own selves. We also find Goddess through meditation and prayer, seeking her "out there." She is the vessel in which creation exists, and also we can find her in our own selves, looking inward and growing toward her. Panentheism describes the dance of Spirit, Soul, Nature, God, Goddess; it is flow; it is holon, something that is both whole and part.

Meditate on the idea of panentheism, which can include finding God in a church, in religion, in the miracle of nature, and in our own soul. Then draw something based on the images and ideas that arose in your meditation. Let your art be meditation and prayer, too.

# January 28

The Denver Zoo saved me. I was a new mom living in a winter-brown city and missing my green homeland. In the middle of January I took my sleep-deprived self and my high-needs infant to the zoo in search of water and greenery. We walked through the steamy tropical house, my baby girl tucked into a front-facing baby carrier (the only way she would ride). We visited the salty smelling sea lions. She squealed and I breathed. Then, when she got sleepy, I would walk laps, waving at the groundskeepers each time we passed.

Zoos have grown a lot since the days of damaged and abused caged animals. Most are dedicated to saving species from extinction, learning about animals, and teaching the public about the natural world. To find one near you, visit www.aza.org.

# January 29

As we move closer to Imbolc, and Yule becomes a more distant memory, we ever so subtly move toward longer days of light. We begin to feel we can celebrate having survived the darkness. Our soul feels not only the triumph of our ancestors, who literally survived the winter, but also the pull of the evolving soul. We all will go through a dark night of the soul, a cleansing of the darkness in our own selves. We will also, eventually, move out of the dark night and into higher levels of consciousness as we move closer to Christ or nondual consciousness. This may take several lifetimes, but our soul knows the journey. About this "resurrection from the Dark Night," theologian Jim Marion writes,

> *After the Dark Night, radical trust becomes*
> *second nature. We understand experientially*
> *not only what faith means, but that the only*
> *sensible way to operate in this world is by means*

*of such radical faith and trust. The universe
we formerly saw as full of threats of every
sort is now seen as a non-threatening place,
one full of gifts, abundance, and blessings.*[25]

That first warm day when you go outside and turn your face to the sun, notice how your soul feels. The soul's journey and the journey of the earth around the sun are parallel stories.

# January 30

> *Relationship in the shamanic sense is dynamic,*
> *coming as it does from a nondual spiritual*
> *concept of the cosmos as a unified movement....*
> *Well-being is not defined through alienating*
> *standards but by participation in Beauty.*
> • • • • • •
> Loren Cruden[26]

Today, bring to your awareness your relationships with people, food, the earth, Spirit. How do you differentiate yourself from these others? What happens when you see yourself as part of a unified movement with these beings? Can you see yourself in your lover, children, the earth? Can you see them in you? On one level, you are separate from the things you dance with—it takes two to tango. On another, there is just the dance.

Draw, sing, or write about this dialectic. We are separate, and we are one. What does this teach you about participation in Beauty?

*Some five billion years after the beginning
of time, the star Tiamat emerged in our spiral
galaxy. Tiamat knit together wonders in its
fiery belly, and then sacrificed itself, carving its
body up in a supernova explosion that dispersed
this new elemental power in all directions,
so that the adventure might deepen.*

Brian Swimme and Thomas Berry, *The Universe Story*[27]

Stars are birthed from supernovas. They move through
the universe, traversing great distances. Some have twin
stars, and others are drawn together and fuse like lovers.
They die, creating greater complexity in the universe.

Stars burn because hydrogen and helium inside them
are attracted to each other. They unite, change, and
birth energy. Stars are great balls of transformation.
Many indigenous people saw stars as living beings. Consider how you define a being or consciousness. Gaze

upon the stars, those alien beings, and witness their part in the unified movement of Beauty.

# February 1

To prepare for Imbolc, which is also the Catholic Candlemas, make candles. Collect old ends of burnt-down candles or buy new wax. Beeswax is more expensive than clear candle wax, but it's worth the cost. Beeswax candles don't put off smoke, and the smell as the wax melts is truly divine and will linger in your kitchen for days. You will also need some heat-proof glass containers or molds, big aluminum cans in which to melt the wax safely in a double boiler, and some wick. Craft stores will have everything you need. For a few resources on candle making, see www.candletech.com, *The Complete Candlemaker* by Norma Coney, and *Creating Candles* by Luisa Sacchi. Local homesteading clubs may also offer classes on making your own candles.

# *Imbolc*

Imbolc means "fire in the belly." The earth is pregnant with spring, which we can just begin to feel around the next corner. Secular America honors this sense with Groundhog Day, not a particularly important holiday (except to Punxsutawney Phil!). But through the Wheel of the Year we do celebrate this time of just awakening. Winter is nearly over, but we are not yet through it. Many of us can still get snow. Others await spring rains. Asparagus has not yet peeked above the soil, but it's coming. We pause, poised between listening inwardly, as we have done through the darkness of the year, and springing forth into the verdant world.

# February 2

The first time a pregnant mother feels the movement of her unborn child is called quickening. During this time of the Wheel we feel the earth begin to quicken, a barely discernible energy of awakening toward spring. Days lengthen, hens lay more eggs, lambs birth in the cold dark of early mornings. Go outside and sit somewhere on the ground if you can, or just stand and feel your feet on the earth. Smell. Feel the earth beneath you. Listen to the birds. Can you feel the humming? The change? Let the wind speak to you. Let it name for you a few things that are coming.

What change or growth lies before you?

## February 3

An expectant mother likes to have something to hold as a material promise that yes, this baby is really coming. She might buy a few key baby clothes, even though her friends have given her all the clothes this baby could ever need. She stands in the nursery, running her hands over the soft crib sheets even if she plans to co-sleep.

We get the same feeling this time of year, longing for the birth of spring. What might you hold in your hands as a talisman for this upcoming birth? A branch brought in from outside may leaf out in the warm house. Pussy willows are a good choice, as they send out their fuzzy catkins. Or perhaps serve a spring salad tonight, using the last winter greens from the cold frame, "springed" up with a little goat cheese and pickled asparagus. If yesterday the wind shared an insight with you, eat your salad with these coming energies in mind. Let the greens or willow branches refresh and guide you into this next phase.

# February 4

On a warm day in early spring (above 60 degrees), bring your houseplants outside and give them a little love. For you this may not happen for a few more months, but some climates allow this—even occasionally—as early as February. Set the plants on the ground without trays underneath and water them deeply, letting the excess run out the bottom of the pot. This flushes salts out of the soil from months of indoor watering. Give them a gentle spray on their leaves to remove dust and cobwebs. Keep them in an area with bright but not direct sunlight. Remember to bring them in before nightfall; freezing temperatures will kill most houseplants, which are primarily from tropical regions.

## February 5

Late winter is the time to trim most woody shrubs and trees (there are a few exceptions, like lilacs, which have already set buds). Consider as you trim that you are removing dead wood or wood that has gotten in the way of the tree's growth. What "dead wood" do you need to trim out of your own life? This might be things or life phases or even relationships that are taking too much of your energy. Consider carefully where to make the cut. Do so when things are dormant. Cut cleanly, with respect for the growth of the main branches. No need to paint over cuts with tar or anything else—the tree knows how to heal. So do you. Letting a tree get too gnarly and overgrown makes it vulnerable to damage from wind and insects. The same is true in your life.

# February 6

Another name for Imbolc is *Oimelc*, meaning "milk of the ewe." Traditionally this was lambing season, when sheep milk begins to flow. Today most sheep farmers control lambing season a little more closely by breeding sheep so the lambs are born later in spring. The energy of Oimelc—the absolute earliest signs of spring peeking through the bitter cold—remains. Sheep and goat milk are easier to digest than cow milk and are higher in nutrients. Many who are lactose intolerant can handle sheep or goat milk. Raw goat milk can help with both diarrhea and constipation, and it helps rebuild intestinal flora.

As our society weans ourselves off fossil fuels, we will need to get our food from smaller farms and smaller animals (see *Eaarth*—yes, that is spelled correctly—by Bill McKibben, page 176). For dinner tonight, include some goat cheese on your pizza or salad. Find a local goat farm and purchase milk or cheese from them, or consider raising goats yourself. See *The Backyard Goat* by Sue Weaver for tips on raising goats even in urban settings.

# February 7

Native American tribes called February Snow Moon, Hunger Moon, and Opening Buds Moon.[28] These names illustrate the in-between time of Imbolc—there is fire, but it's "in the belly." We feel the quickening of the very first buds of spring, but it's still snowy, and the nourishing crops are a long way off.

Today, clear out your pantry to make room for spring. Throw out and recycle stale boxes of crackers and old cereal. Identify those bags of odd grains and devise some recipes to use them up. Soup is a great way to use a small amount of just about any grain. If you find any nonperishables like macaroni and cheese or canned goods that you probably won't eat, bring them to a food pantry to help others who may be suffering from hunger, even in these modern times.

# February 8

The Old English name for February was *solmonað*, meaning "mud month."[29] Mud may be a nuisance, sticking to our boots and splattering the car, but it is a powerful marriage of water, earth, and a little fire to melt winter's ice. Scoop some mud into your hands, or just soil if you haven't any mud, and feel it. What story does it tell? Where did the rain or snow that fell to make mud come from? How was this soil formed—by rocks, a river, layers of leaf litter? Squish the mud between your fingers. What is its texture? Smell?

We'll revisit mud in a few weeks. For today, just get to know the quality of your mud and how it informs your own *solmonað*.

# February 9

At Imbolc, the Goddess is still a maiden, a young woman not yet married. She prepares for her commitment to the God, which happens at Beltane. This is a time to contemplate your next phase of commitment. In the phase between the business of winter holidays and the bustle of spring planting, there is a lull when we are like maidens or youth. We are no longer naive children and not yet responsible adults. In many traditional cultures, this time was marked by a coming of age ceremony, an initiation. The initiate is not yet an adult, not yet an adept, but is just beginning to understand the path she or he walks.

In what ways do you feel like an initiate or maiden/youth? Look for objects that represent the path you think you may be initiated into. Perhaps a job change looms or you're contemplating raising chickens in the spring or you have been dating someone but haven't committed more deeply to the relationship yet. What images or objects could represent this upcoming deepening? Gather them and place them on your altar, perhaps, or journal about your status as an initiate.

## February 10

Gather some seeds, crystals, and herbs you feel drawn
to working with. Set them on a clean cloth and smudge
them by wafting over them smoke from sage, cedar, or
another herb. Dedicate these objects to your personal
goals and the goals of your community. These might
include purification, healing, connection, revitalization, or strength. Sit in prayer and dedication, sending
your intentions into these objects and asking them for
their blessings. Let yourself align with the sacred truths
of the herbs, stones, and seeds chosen for this purpose.
When you feel a shift of energy as your intentions and
the sacred truths of the objects align, ground yourself,
thank the objects, and put them in a little bag or wrap
them in cloth. Set the cloth or bag on your altar. We will
revisit them later.

Make your own birdseed block by dissolving 1 ounce of unflavored gelatin into ¼ cup water in a pan over low heat. When the water is clear, remove from heat and stir in 1¼ cups high-quality birdseed mix. White millet, black oil sunflower, dried fruit, and peanuts are all good choices. Press the mixture into a container (like a large, empty yogurt container) and chill till set. Remove from the container and put in a mesh bag like the kind you get onions in from the store, and hang the bag from a tree or set as-is on a feeder made for seed blocks. A seed block lasts longer than bulk seed and will attract a wide variety of birds, depending on what you put in the block.

# February 12

Commercially grown roses use huge amounts of chemicals, fertilizers, and water to produce, and as with most commercial agriculture are often grown by exploited workers. This Valentine's Day, give your love local flowers or potted plants from trusted sources. Also look for Fair Trade roses; talk to your local florist about carrying them, then write a letter to the local paper and on your social networking sites to inform people of why this florist carries superior roses. The extra price is worth it to the environment and to plantation workers.

Another option is to make paper roses or other flowers that will last longer than real. For one idea, see http://www.marthastewart.com/266346/paper-roses. The book *Paper Blossoms* by Ray Marshall is a pop-up book and changeable centerpiece. *Paper Bouquet* by Susan Tierney Cockburn is a guide to making flowers using paper punches.

## February 13

Purchase Fair Trade-certified chocolate this Valentine's Day. "Most chocolate sold in the US comes from cocoa farms where farmers work in unsafe conditions [and] receive below-poverty wages, many of them children under fourteen years old who are forced to work and denied education," writes Tex Dworkin of the Global Exchange Fair Trade Online Store.[30] After supporting Fair Trade, visit http://www.raisethebarhershey.org/ to join the campaign working to get Hershey to remove child labor from its chocolate production.

# February 14

The heart generates an electric field sixty times stronger than the brain, a field that can be detected several feet away from the body.[31] Electric fields want to entrain with each other, or synchronize into complementary wave lengths. Your heart vibrations affect those around you. This is part of the reason why being around someone who is happy will raise your mood and why fear spreads quickly. It also may be part of why depression, loneliness, and social isolation can contribute to heart disease.[32] Strengthen your heart—and the people and animals around you—by breathing light into your heart center. Follow your breath, feel your heart beat, and focus on calm, lightening energy. Know that you are not only creating better health in yourself but also in those with whom you interact.

Bird songs slowed down to one-quarter speed reveal that what we hear as a blur of sound is chock-full of information to birds. Chickadees, wrens, robins, and other songbirds have complex chirps and songs, the complexity of which we cannot appreciate until we slow it down (the same is true of crickets—see June 17). They can pack a lot of information into a short bit of song. "Creatures with which we share the world read and respond to nature in ways we sometimes cannot see or hear," reminds Todd Peterson in his piece on the winter wren for NPR's *BirdNote*, available online at http://birdnote.org/show/what-birds-can-hear-songs.

As you listen to birds, close your eyes and really listen deeply. What can you hear? What does it evoke in you?

# February 16

It's skunk mating season! This means these cocky creatures, who have no known predators, will be trying to
cross roads more often—so drive with extra care. Skunk
energy is about reputation and respect. When we carry
ourselves erect as a skunk tail, we radiate self-respect,
and this is communicated to others. Asserting the self
without ego can be challenging for many people, yet
learning to do so is key to creating and maintaining
healthy relationships. Examine what energy you are putting out to others to see how you are helping to create
your current situation.[33]

# February 17

This month is named for the Latin *februum,* meaning "purification," after a Roman feast of purification held mid-February. The month was not part of the original Roman calendar but was added about 713 BCE by Numa Pompilius.[34] The early Romans saw winter as having no months. Sometimes in the midst of February it feels this way—adrift in the chill that will never end, a chill that purifies us down to nothing.

Purify by taking deep, cleansing breaths, pushing out all the old air at the end of your exhale. Avoid sugar for the day, and eat only small amounts of animal products. Feel yourself releasing any energies that are blocking you from your purest self.

# February 18

Water energy and rebirth are the aspects of the Celtic month of Nion, named for ash, a sacred Druid tree. The sun god Lugh, whose sabbat Lughnassah sits opposite Imbolc on the Wheel, had a magical spear of ash.

Before you can be reborn, you must rest in stillness in the womb. Today, take some time to rest in a "womb"— your bed piled with blankets or a warm bath with a little sea salt in a dark bathroom or, perhaps, a sweat lodge— any dark, warm, safe place. Meditate on how the spear of Lugh, which relates to the magic wand of modern magic, might help you direct your own energies at this time. Journal, dream, and float. When you're ready, rise from the bath or the pile of blankets, and allow your newly directed energy to be reborn.

## February 19

The sun enters Pieces today, the last sign in the zodiac. This watery sign, represented by the fish, is creative, dreamy, and sensitive. Spend some time making art today. This could be finger painting or oil on canvas, writing poetry or composing silly Facebook posts, or dancing to your favorite music. Let your intuition and watery self guide you.

Creativity is a very nature-oriented process, for it aligns us with the innate creative energy of the natural world. Painting, ceramics, gardening, cooking, writing with a wooden pencil—all of these engage the senses and utilize naturally derived supplies. Delve into creation.

# February 20

As you plan your garden, consider your plant allies. What plants that grow in your climate—either cultivated or wild—do you feel a special kinship with? These plants might show up in dreams, grow unexpectedly alongside your house, or appear throughout your life in specific experiences. For me, one of these plants is nettle, which I grew up with in the Pacific Northwest. I work with dried nettle now that I cannot grow it here in Colorado (it does grow in some places here, but not in my yard, no matter how hard I try). The unassuming weed mallow speaks to me also. It grows throughout my yard, and I work with it for soothing, strengthening, and nourishing.

Whatever plants you feel drawn to, keep in mind that they are beings worthy of respect. Shamanic herbalist Loren Cruden writes, "Plant allies are teachers who do not always behave with the passivity expected of rooted, vegetative beings."[35]

Invite your allies into your garden with respect and curiosity. By approaching plants as teachers and allies, we create a living, sacred world.

# February 21

Before mason bees and bumblebees come out of winter dormancy, hang houses for them in your yard. Both bees provide pollination and are gentle bees that rarely sting. Mason bees are not social bees but nest in long, hollow tubes. They use pollen and mud to make their nests, so providing a mud source near the nest box in spring can aid the mother bees.

Bumblebees are large, fuzzy, social bees. They nest in tree cavities or the ground. You can also create bumblebee houses out of large coffee cans (search "bumblebee house coffee can"). Put them out in spring to attract a new colony.

Local nurseries may sell mason bee and bumblebee houses, or buy them online at www.gardeners.com. Instructions for making a mason bee nest block can be found at familyfun.go.com/crafts/bee-house-876193/.

## February 22

Humans have been baking bread for thousands of years. Bread unites the energies of earth (flour), air (rising), water, and fire. A cold February day is a great time to bake bread using your favorite recipe. When I ate gluten, I liked the tasty simplicity of Mollie Katzen's focaccia recipe in her *Moosewood Cookbook*. For a great gluten-free recipe, check out the fabulous Gluten Free Girl, both the cookbook and the blog—glutenfreegirl.com.

As you make bread—whether you throw the ingredients into a bread maker, knead flour/water/yeast the old-fashioned way, or mix up a gluten-free batter—consider the history of these grains going back thousands of years, touched by the hands of countless generations of farmers, watered by rain and irrigation systems. Enter wonder and thanks for how this moment connects you with the whole planet.

# February 23

A fabulous resource for learning about urban nature is the blog www.thenatureofcities.com. It is a compendium of essays by nature writers and scientists about cities as ecological spaces. Topics include transforming abandoned lots, creating biodiversity, and designing cities to better support interaction with animals, plants, and the elements. Essays are open to comments. You can sign up for an RSS feed or just poke around the site to get inspired. Then head out to a local city park, trail, or waterway, and see what February has to offer.

# February 24

*"The connectedness that blossoms through
such experiences brings with it the gift of
at-home-ness on Earth—the trust that loving
resource embodies itself throughout life."*
. . . . . .
Loren Cruden[36]

Connecting directly with nature in the city, in the wilderness, in the garden, and in your daily life creates a sense of relationship and connection. In this connection we can find that sense of *home* we humans seem to find so elusive. The powerful dialectic of ecospirituality is that we are at home on this planet *and* we are at home in spirit. Remember Jim Marion's words: "The universe we formerly saw as full of threats of every sort is now seen as a non-threatening place, one full of gifts, abundance, and blessings."[37] Interesting how both Marion's and Cruden's quotes speak of a similar sense of faith and safety in the universe. Sit in prayer today, connecting with this sense of home in nature and spirit.

IMBOLC

# February 25

Around this date Japan and China celebrate the emergence of plum blossoms, among the very first signs of spring. The plum blossom is a symbol of early spring, strength, and peace. "Zhu Xi, a noted Song Dynasty Confucian scholar, gave the plum four virtues: the great potential in the bud, prosperity in the flower, harmony in the fruit, and rightness in its maturity—all of which embody the characteristics of heaven (*qian*), according to the Book of Change. Chinese also see the five-petaled flower as symbolizing five blessings: longevity, prosperity, health, virtue, and good living," writes Hong Jiang.[38]

What early signs of spring do you see in your climate? Record them by writing about them or photographing what you discover. Align with their energies and their sacred truths, such as longevity, hope, and harmony.

## February 26

Get a jump on the outdoor growing season by starting tomato, basil, and strawberry seeds indoors. An ecological potting soil alternative is dairy fiber, composted manure from milk dairies (see http://www.highwayfuel.com/pp_dairy_fiber.html); ask your local plant nursery if they can carry it. Keep seeds evenly moist and covered with plastic (reuse produce bags) until they sprout. Fertilize with a little organic fertilizer when they come up. Indoor seedlings need many hours of bright light. Use a grow table or, if you only have a few pots or trays, a couple flexible-neck desk lamps with CFL bulbs will also do the trick.

# February 27

This is a good time of year to hang a bat house so that it will be ready for occupants when they come looking for homes in spring. Bats eat insects and are key members of ecosystems. They teach us about letting go of the ego and traveling between worlds. In most areas of the United States, bat houses should be painted dark. They need direct sun exposure—don't hang it in a tree. Mount a bat house on a pole or side of your house at least twelve feet above the ground; fifteen to twenty feet is better. For more information and free building plans, see Bat Conservation International's website at www .batcon.org.

## February 28

The nutrient content and tilth, or fluffiness, of soil determines the health of your garden. Nutrients in the soil will be taken up by your plants and then by you. Even in organic gardening, which puts nutrients into the soil without the use of heavy petrochemical-based fertilizers, soil must be rebuilt in some way after the plants remove the soil's micronutrients. Cover crops, compost, blood meal, ground-up shells—these are all ways of replenishing the soil. Feed the soil; that feeds the plants. Today, even before you have planted the garden in most temperate zones, perform a ritual of thanks and blessing on the soil. Even if you don't garden, take some time to thank the soil for nourishing you. Pray, sing, sprinkle some of your hair on the earth, and speak your gratitude to the complex world we call soil.

## March 1

*Imbolc* means "fire in the belly," a time when the Goddess is pregnant with life not yet sprouted. When I was pregnant with each of my children, I went crazy with the nesting instinct. I moved, redecorated, ripped up carpet, built a chicken coop, hauled mulch...

What nesting instincts are stirring in you right now? Take twenty minutes or more today cleaning a closet, dusting the top of the refrigerator, or organizing your desk. Feel the energy released when you tackle these chores—especially ones you have been avoiding. Later we will revisit spring cleaning, which usually takes longer than a day. For today, focus on what your home is asking you to do and what nesting instinct is taking over as spring energy grows.

# March 2

Get yourself some crayons if you haven't any already, and peel the paper off a few colors. Gather drawing paper. Go for a walk anywhere that has a variety of trees—an arboretum, botanic garden, park, or the forest behind your house, if you are so lucky. Take rubbings by pressing the paper against tree bark and rubbing the crayon flat against the paper. You can also create leaf rubbings; put a piece of cardboard or a book behind a leaf and cover with your paper rather than removing the leaf from the tree (or gather them off the ground). If you know the name of the tree, you can label your rubbings or later use the rubbing to help identify the tree. Or just let the shapes and textures speak for themselves. What do they tell you about the tree?

# March 3

One of the earliest spring herbs is parsley. If you started some indoors in the last few months, or if you have access to early farmers' markets, gather a big bunch to make parsley pesto. You can use store-bought parsley, but it's rarely as flavorful. Mix two cups fresh parsley with a half cup of walnuts, a clove or two of garlic, a teaspoon of salt, and a few tablespoons of olive or coconut oil. Blend till smooth, adding water if needed to make a smooth pesto. Toss with hot pasta and a little reserved pasta water, and top with Parmesan if desired.

Early spring flowers like pansies, crocuses, daffodils, and lilacs all tend to be yellow and purple. Blue, purple, and yellow flowers are the most attractive to bees; they see them as blue. According to color therapy, yellow is associated with mental clarity, memory, and confidence. Violet connects us to our spiritual self and to inspiration, creativity, and beauty.[39] Perhaps spring is about marrying mental realms with spiritual energy, giving us energy (yellow) to pursue our spiritual calling (purple). Collect or buy a bouquet of spring flowers to energize and soothe.

# March 5

If you are prone to seasonal allergies or are just feeling depleted, include some stinging nettles in your diet. Nettles contain small amounts of histamine, and they help the body prepare for and build strength against hayfever. Pick them young (wear gloves) and cook them with pasta or add them to soup (when you cook them, they lose their sting). If you live somewhere they do not grow, buy dried or freeze-dried nettle and take as tea or capsules. The tea can be very warming and even cause nausea if too strong; mix with raspberry leaf or red clover to mellow it out a little.

# March 6

When you look at a tree, you see only the half above ground. An extensive root system lives underground, away from our eyes and, therefore, usually out of our awareness. The root system takes in water and, through this water, nutrients. Roots anchor the tree. They even communicate with other trees nearby through chemical exchange.

Branching roots and branches maximize surface area, as in many other circulatory systems like blood, lungs, and rivers. This form, seen throughout nature, is constantly moving nutrients, water, and air.

Stand beneath a tree and see in your mind's eye the branches and the roots beneath you. See your body's own river systems of flowing energy. Feel the connections between you and the tree.

# March 7

Every fruit has its own pattern and rhythm. Cut an apple in half horizontally to find a five-pointed star. Watermelons are divided into three sections, each of which has two little globs inside, making it a six (like frozen water!). Oranges often have ten sections. Once I started looking for the patterns and numbers in cross-sections of fruit, I became a little obsessed with it. I'm not sure how the patterns relate to numerology, but there must be evolutionary and energetic reasons behind the patterns. Many fruits and flowers follow the Fibonacci sequence: 1, 1, 2, 3, 5, 8, 13 ...

Cross-section some fruit today. For more on numbers and their significance (outside of numerology or Kabala), see *A Beginner's Guide to Constructing the Universe* by Michael S. Schneider.

As soon as the rains clear, go play in the mud. Let your inner child—and your inner sculptor—play. Find the edge of a mud puddle or a garden bed you haven't yet planted, and mix it with rainwater or a little tap water. Make clay. Squish and sculpt, mash and roll. What does the texture and smell of the mud teach you about your soil?

In Genesis and in Lakota creation myths, people were formed out of clay or mud. What are you creating—not just in this mud you play with, but in your own life? How does playing in mud inform this process?

# March 9

Certify your backyard as a wildlife habitat—or just build one without getting a certificate from the National Wildlife Federation. To become a certified wildlife habitat, you need four elements: food, water, cover, and a place to raise young. Seeds, berries, flowers, and nuts provide food. Water can be provided by a bird bath, pond, or stream. Shrubs, birdhouses, dead and living trees, and brush piles provide both shelter and places to raise young.

If you want to certify, for which you pay a small fee and receive a certificate, visit the National Wildlife Federation's website at http://www.nwf.org/Get-Outside/Outdoor-Activities/Garden-for-Wildlife/Create-a -Habitat.aspx.

# March 10

Why is gardening so important? Gardening is a relationship with the earth. It is a co-creative process whereby you put a little stonelike thing into dirt and, with a little water and a little sun, you get food in return. Picture the smile on a child's face when she harvests a tomato that she helped grow, and you know the power of the garden. Growing your own food means you have power and self-efficacy. Even in the poorest parts of the world, where there isn't enough money for regular electricity or to get shoes for a community's children, gardens grow. They represent life and hope. And in the richest parts of the world, like the White House and Prince Charles's Highgrove Estate, a garden is a reminder that we depend on nature, that small gestures matter, and that we are all interconnected.

So whether you homestead ten acres or plant basil seeds in a pot on your windowsill, to truly connect with the land, you need a garden.

# March 11

Hold a plant in your hand, any plant. Try to picture its energy processes: the sun and water and carbon dioxide it turns into life, supported by the fungal and bacterial waste in soil and the minerals of five billion years' worth of stone and mineral. Visualize its roots exchanging nutrients as the leaves exchange gases. Go back in time into the seed that formed it—into that mother and father plant, into the wind or animal that carried the seed to the spot where it grew. Sit with the pedigree of this plant for several moments, feeling this one moment spread back through time and space.

# March 12

*"The voice of the Lord is upon the waters; the God of glory thunders; the Lord is upon many waters."*
......
Psalm 29

When we stand beside a waterfall or peer out into the deluge of a thunderstorm or hear the roar of a flash flood or ocean waves, this is one of the voices of the Goddess. The Divine speaks to us through many waters.

Listen deeply to a rainstorm, an ocean, or a river. Close your eyes. Let yourself enter the sound, and let the sound enter you.

# March 13

If the time feels right, return to the bag of seeds, crystals, and herbs on your altar. Sit outside with the bag. Hold it in your hand and reengage with the intentions you set on February 10. Feel the vibration of the beings in your bag. Open the bag and pray over the objects, rededicating yourself to these intentions you had stated for yourself and your community. Take the objects to a sacred place—the base of a tree in your yard, the four corners of your property, a flower pot in the courtyard of your apartment building—somewhere that calls to you. Give thanks and prayer to the objects, then bury them in this sacred place. Finish by thanking the space for helping you send your intentions into the earth. Smudge yourself when finished; the smoke will bring your intentions and your ritual into the realm of air.

# March 14

A cairn is a human-made pile or stack of stones. Traditionally they have been constructed to mark burial sites or sacred pathways. Today, you can find piles of stones in rivers and along mountain pathways, built as meditations to attune with the spirit of the river. While the builders may not use the words *spirit* and *meditation*, that is, essentially, what they are doing. Balancing the stones takes precision, attention, and diligence. With your feet in the river and your hands hoisting rocks, you become a part of the river. Try building your own cairn at a river, in your garden, or just off the path on a hike. Note that some parks have regulations against building structures of any sort, so you may want to inquire first.

# March 15

Using a cup of dirt from your backyard—or the backyard of a friend who lives nearby if you're in an apartment—make a mineral mud mask. Mix with warmed, filtered water till it's the consistency of cake frosting. Add herbs (lavender, sage, lemon balm) from the yard if desired. Gently smear on your face—go slow and gentle, for some dirt can be very gritty. As it sits, deeply feel the mud, and let it soak into your soul as well as your skin. Let set till it starts to crack, then wash off with a bowl of warm water outside (I don't recommend washing it off in the bath or sink, as it will clog the drains). Wash skin with a gentle, natural cleanser, then moisturize. Give thanks to your land for its gift.

# March 16

> *This grand show is eternal. It is always sunrise*
> *somewhere; the dew is never all dried at once;*
> *a shower is forever falling; vapor is ever rising.*
> *Eternal sunrise, eternal sunset, eternal dawn*
> *and gloaming, on sea and continents and islands,*
> *each in its turn, as the round earth rolls.*
> • • • • • •
> John Muir[40]

Read the above quote a few times, then close your eyes and settle into its images and meaning. Record your thoughts and feelings in your journal.

# March 17

Based on zone 5's last average frost date of May 10, on St. Patrick's Day I can plant peas. For many areas you will already have begun the spring garden; if you have not done so, plant a few seeds today (it's not too late, even in warmer zones). Peas, spinach, lettuces, carrots, and kale are all great spring cool-season crops. They all do well in pots and planters as well as raised beds and general garden soil. Check the back of the seed packet: if it says plant in early spring, it's a cool-season crop. If it says to wait till danger of frost has passed, then you probably need to wait (depending, of course, on your climate). For planting dates, consult a planting chart by zone (consult your local extension office), and also consider the moon phase and sign by consulting this year's *Llewellyn's Moon Sign Book* (http://www.llewellyn.com).

The Celtic month of Fearn, called *Gwernen* in Welsh, begins today. It is named for the alder tree, bringing the aspects of fire energy, warriorship, and action. Spring is in full swing in most parts of the Northern Hemisphere, in whatever way spring is expressed where you live. The name *spring* is an action, moving upward quickly. Pay attention to what projects in your life are ready to spring forth, and identify three actions you can take today to make these projects come to fruition. Or journal about how you are called to warriorship at this time: what are you protecting or fighting for? Call on alder to help your work.

# Ostara

Ostara is celebrated in the Northern Hemisphere somewhere between March 19 and 22, depending on the vernal equinox. It is named for the German goddess of spring, Ostara. The secular Easter symbols of eggs, rabbits, pastel colors, fresh grass, and baby chicks all originate with Ostara traditions centered around the rebirth of spring. This is a time to seek balance, as day and night are equal, and to prepare for the bursting forth of spring.

For the next six weeks we will plant seeds, clean out the cobwebs, and let in the light. We seek pollination for our projects. This is a time to feel young again and to delight in the flowering of the land.

## March 19

To celebrate Ostara, plant seeds. Depending on your climate, you can plant in the garden or start seeds indoors. Try planting parsley or lettuce in pots to set in a sunny windowsill or put out on the deck. If you haven't already, start tomato or pepper seeds indoors to put out in the garden after the danger of frost has passed. Easy seeds for beginners or children include radishes and marigolds. For those whose frost dates have already passed, you can put anything you like out in the garden.

Whatever seeds you choose, hold them in your hands before planting. Project your awareness into them, tuning in to their inner wisdom carried down from plant to plant over thousands of years. Send love and intention to them. Press them into moist potting soil, and water them with water into which you've radiated love and gratitude. Ask the devas to ground the energy of whatever you plant into your garden. Give thanks.

# March 20

Ostara is also known as the spring (or vernal) equinox, when day and night are (roughly) equal. This time of year is about balance. Today, practice a few yoga poses that focus on balance. If the weather permits, do them outside. Begin by standing on both feet. Breathe all the way down into your feet, and then into the earth. Try tree pose: stand on one foot, with the other pressed against your thigh and your hands over your head. Another balancing pose is crow pose: lean forward onto your hands, resting your knees on your bent elbows.

For any balancing pose, pick a spot a few feet in front of you to focus your eyes upon. Let your gaze go soft. Let your mind quiet. Let the feeling of being balanced inform your daily life as you seek balance in all you do.

## March 21

The sun enters the astrological sign of Aries on or around March 21, beginning the astrological year. Aries is about force, fire, and outgoing energy.[41] There is a "me first" attitude, as well as fiery enthusiasm, to Aries. Notice in what areas of your life you are feeling fiery and forceful. Does this energy serve others or is it a selfish burst of fire? To live in harmony with others—and the earth—we must ignite and follow our passions while helping others to do the same. We must balance selfcare with care for others. Journal about how these energies play out in your life at this time. Ask the stars for guidance in finding both balance and passion.

# March 22

If you are blessed to live in a climate that brings spring rain, leave out a little cup to collect the falling water. This water has existed since the beginning of water on earth, traveling along its cycle from ocean to sky to mountain to river and back to sky. This rain may have helped cool electrical equipment at a power production facility or flushed waste down a toilet or plumped a carrot or fought a fire. It returned again to the swish and flight of water droplets, evaporated, froze, and was pulled back toward the center of the earth.

Hold your cup of rainwater or just stand in the rain and meditate on how the planet's water and its gravitational field are constantly playing with each other, making life on earth possible.

# March 23

In Chinese medicine, spring is ruled by the wood element. It is a time of rising energies, like blades of grass rising upward, and of emotional and physical cleansing. This is a time to attend to the liver and the gallbladder, and to eat lighter meals than in winter. Young plants, fresh greens, raw food, and sprouts all aid in cleansing and lightening. Raw onions and garlic can cleanse the body of parasites. Cooking food for short times and at high temperatures retains spring's vitality. Tonight, stir-fry baby root vegetables and serve with sprouted or soaked rice and spring greens.

# March 24

Some of the seeds you planted on the 19<sup>th</sup> will have germinated, but many may not have done so. Each plant has its own needs concerning light, temperature, and moisture. Some germinate quickly—like amenable, easy radishes—while others, like carrots, are picky about moisture and light. Some just take time to wake up.

Germinate more seeds today, but this time in damp paper towels. Beans, tomatoes, and pumpkin seeds are good candidates for this treatment, as they are fairly large and prefer darkness to germinate. Put a few seeds in a damp paper towel and tuck into a plastic bag. Label the bag with a permanent marker and set it in a slightly warm place—on top of your water heater is a good spot. We'll check back in a few days.

# March 25

Animals don't plant seeds to reproduce; they make eggs. Both seeds and eggs must be fertilized to create the next generation. Eggs and seeds all contain nutrients designed to feed the baby until it can gain nutrients from the greater world. All eggs and seeds carry a packet of genetic information informing their precious cargo of who they are and how to carry out their unique assignment of being.

This time of year you see many egg images. In the materialism of Easter we may become detached from the powerful meaning of the egg. As you encounter eggs today, hold in mind the metaphor and message of the egg: the promise of new life and the hope that comes with that promise. This is a message that transcends and unites religions.

# March 26

Meditation for today:

Imagine yourself encased in a thick shell. It surrounds you, round, smooth, and safe. You are tightly curled into yourself inside a little egg. All nutrition has always been provided by the primal substance in which you float. Now you begin to feel a humming sensation, a pulling. You try to unfold your tightly curled body. You cannot. For the first time, your shell feels tight, constricting. You wiggle and push, tapping at the shell with your single egg tooth. You hear and feel a tiny crack forming. The sensation frightens you but also fills you with excitement and a sense of purpose. You poke at the crack. It widens. Your heart pounds inside your tiny body. The crack turns into a hole, through which you see light. You pause. What could this light be? It calls to you. You wiggle and poke and make the hole larger, until suddenly your shell cracks! You unfold your body, triumphant and

a little stunned. Your shell lies next to you in pieces, no longer needed. You look around at the world you have entered.

What do you see?

# March 27

Open the windows and wash them, dust, clean out the fridge, and vacuum beneath the bed. To get dust mites out of your mattress, let your kids (or yourself) jump on the bed (with no bedding on), then vacuum.

The fabulous *Little House in the Suburbs* offers the following recipe for a tough multipurpose cleaner:

> 2 tablespoons vinegar
> 1 teaspoon borax
> 2 cups hot water
> 2 tablespoons to ¼ cup castile soap
>     (depending on desired strength)
> 10–15 drops essential oil such as
>     lemon or lavender

Combine vinegar, borax, and hot water in a spray bottle and shake well till borax is dissolved. Add soap and essential oil and swirl. Use when you need a strong multipurpose cleaner, like once a week on the kitchen counters or scrubbing around the toilet bowl.[42]

When your house is physically clean, smudge with a white sage bundle or a favorite incense. Waft the smoke into corners and over doorways, holding the intention that this smudge will cleanse the energy of your home.

# March 28

Check the seeds we started in paper towels. Pull them out of the bag and gently open the paper towel. Many of the seeds will have germinated, sending out long, white roots. Some might even have sent out baby leaves, too. Notice how the roots seek out nutrients and the leaves, the light. The way they grow reminds me of an infant rooting for the breast, searching back and forth for that sweet spot of nourishment.

Your germinated seeds can now be gently moved to potting soil and given light. This is a great way to germinate older seeds like tomatoes from two years ago; only the ones that germinate will be planted. Keep these and your other seedlings evenly moist, and provide sixteen hours or more of bright light. Grow lights or even just a couple of CFL bulbs in gooseneck lamps will do the trick. A sunny window doesn't provide enough light and can cause them to get leggy and weak.

# March 29

To shift to being an earth- and life-affirming species, we must create "a worldview in which our deep kinship with others, both human and nonhuman, is acknowledged and honored," writes Thom van Dooren in *Pagan Visions for a Sustainable Future*.[43] Spring is a great time to notice and affirm our kinship with others. Most of us don't raise, hunt, or catch our own meat on a regular basis; gardening is more accessible and manageable for most people. When you pluck a pea from the garden grown by the power of sunlight, water, and Spirit, you experience the interconnection of everything. You are also taking a life so that you may live.

Today—whether you pick a radish, eat meat, or consume the seed of a pea plant—consider that life is gifted to you "by the death of others."[44] This is not a "sin," it is simply the way of the world. Accept that gift with humble and aware gratitude. Give something back by adding strands of your hair or nail clippings to the compost pile.

# March 30

Things are sprouting and unfolding, spring-green and full of life.

Journal topic for today: What is pushing through the soil for you right now? What has been in darkness and is now seeking the light? How can you nourish this unfolding energy? As you write, tap into the hum of the earth and let it guide you.

# March 31

A study of American life in the twenty-first century by a team of anthropologists and archaeologists found that many Americans simply have too much stuff.[45] This attachment to stuff—and the space to store our stuff—fuels long hours of work and preparation for work, such as school, homework, and sports, all of which make us too busy to go outside. It weighs us down.

Go through your closets, drawers, garage, toy box, and book shelves. Get rid of anything you don't use that doesn't have significant sentimental value. Clothes that don't fit or you haven't worn, old toys no longer played with, books you've already read, kitchen gadgets you've used twice—load it all up and donate it to a secondhand store. Be ruthless. You are making room for new energy, new life. You are making room for a real relationship with the land.

Many people cannot get rid of their clutter because they identify with stuff. It makes us feel secure, known. When you get rid of a bunch of stuff, it can feel freeing, but it can also feel vulnerable. If you're feeling hesitant to clear out the clutter or feeling emotional now that you have done so, send compassion to that part of you that is afraid or grieving. These emotions contain kernels of truth about who you believe yourself to be. Send them love and compassion, and the darkness will dissolve while the truth is brought to light.

In order to push through the soil and toward the light, you must release the past. You can move forward unencumbered if you let go of what you no longer need.

# April 2

A last bit on spring cleaning: you can recycle almost anything. Batteries and light bulbs can be recycled at hardware stores. Bring empty print cartridges and old electronics to electronic and office supply stores. In Denver and some other cities, one can actually get paid a few cents a pound for old carpet, carpet pad, and metal at their respective recycling centers. Clothes and shoes, when too worn for the secondhand store, can be recycled into insulation; look in parking lots for bins that say "recycle clothes and shoes here."

Recycling honors the fact that we are all interconnected. Our waste can get piled up in polluting landfills or it can be repurposed. Take today to set up curbside recycling if you haven't already, and look for places to recycle the junk you have sitting around. Search online using the terms "[whatever you need to recycle] [your city] recycling."

# April 3

In November we examined the Via Negativa, the path to Goddess through stillness, suffering, and darkness. Today we look at the Via Positiva, theologian Matthew Fox's first path in Creation Spirituality. "In the awe, wonder, nature, and mystery of all beings, each of whom is a 'word of God,' 'a mirror of God that glistens and glitters,' as Hildegard of Bingen put it," we awaken to the power of Spirit.[46] This is also known as "Thou Shalt Fall in Love at Least Three Times a Day."[47]

Go outside and walk, opening your heart, until something catches your eye or calls to you: a leaf, a flower, a stone, a tree. Sit with that thing, that "word of God," and let yourself fall in love. You do this by being with this thing, this leaf or river or feather or stone. You sit and witness and let it speak to you, and you will fall in love. In doing so, you will better understand Goddess and your own deep nature.

## April 4

> *And forget not that the earth delights*
> *to feel your bare feet and the winds*
> *long to play with your hair.*
> • • • • • •
> Kahlil Gibran, *The Prophet*[48]

Our culture is loath to attribute personality or consciousness to nature, for we've been taught that the scientific method and a scientific way of viewing the world is the only "true" path to knowledge. We fear backsliding toward a primitive way of seeing the world, as if that perspective lacked all value. But there is a difference between a prerational view of the world, before "science," and a transrational view, a way of relating that includes and transcends a purely scientific, rational perspective.

Let yourself play with the wind. Let your attention rise and dip with the wind, letting it teach you about itself. Notice the sense of joy that comes not just from you, but from the wind and the trees and the land.

# April 5

Let the spring cleanup of your yard be a devotion. Approach the raking, fertilizing, watering, and trimming in the way you would the washing of another person's feet. Set an intention before you begin to offer your work in service of the land. Greet the spring blossoms. Lovingly stroke green buds sprouting on the trees. Turn the compost as you would change a church altar cloth. End with a moment of silence and thanks.

# April 6

Something happens within us when we act with compassion for others no matter their size, shape, or life path. When you give your neighbor a few eggs from your hens or some spring greens just to share the gift of the garden, you feel a sense of grace. We act compassionately not to be righteous but simply because the grace of courtesy and compassion has moved us. What small act of kindness can you offer today?

# April 7

*"The garden isn't, at its best, designed for admiration or praise; it leads to an appreciation of the natural universe and to a meditation on the connection between the self and the rest of the natural universe."*

Stanley Kunitz[49]

Our culture has a tendency to want to control—to create straight lines and definable boundaries. But it's in the messy parts—the weeds, the overgrown pear tree, the jumble of blackberries—that magic happens. It is here, smeared with mud and a little bit sunburned, that we know our place in the natural universe.

Find a garden not designed for admiration or praise, but one for knowing the universe. Play, explore, and let yourself feel that deep connection.

# April 8

> *"We could fall in love*
> *with a galaxy every day."*
> • • • • • •
> Matthew Fox[50]

Write a list today of all the things you love—truly love—
that are not people or pets. The oak tree outside your
window, the smell of rain, the sight of the first star at
dusk. What things move you so deeply you feel centered
in yourself and pulled toward God in the same instant?

# April 9

We exist because space exists. Because of the perfect pull of the moon, which reduces the wobble of the earth, keeping our climates relatively stable. Because of Jupiter's great mass, which deflects many large bodies from colliding with the earth. Because our planet is poised at just the right distance from a perfectly sized star. We exist because the universe created a planet in a solar system in a galaxy in a universe just right.

Write a song or paint or pray or just sit with the energy this realization brings to you.

# April 10

Trees do more than provide shade, wood, and fruit. They transform many forms of energy. They turn sunlight into stored fuel. They act as wind barriers and "convert wind action into 'soil stirring' through their roots, aerating the earth for other plants."[52] They collect soil runoff, trap precipitation, and help increase rain and fog. Trees transpire stored precipitation, returning it to the atmosphere. Planting trees stabilizes soil, rain, and energy. It reduces carbon dioxide and pollution. Plant a tree today, or help someone else do so. Notice the roots, branches, bark, and other aspects of the tree; also be aware of the soil into which you plant, and consider how all these aspects will dynamically interact with each other over the next many years.

# April 11

In a culture that fears the messiness of nature, it can feel alienating to become a person who sees the Goddess in the natural world. When you find that gardening, raising chickens, putting solar panels on your house, and seeking the company of wild things have become your center, you may feel that others don't quite understand. And when you begin to weave different spiritual strands into a great garment under which you feel closest to the Divine, you may similarly find yourself feeling alone and misunderstood.

Seek out allies and community through Unitarian churches, healing centers, yoga studios, community gardens, and spiritual book stores. You may also be surprised to find that most people, despite their upbringing and fears, will relate to you on certain key points. Be open to others being open, and magic can happen.

# April 12

Some strains of conservationism have preached the idea that our goal in environmental restoration is to return the earth to the pristine Eden it must have been before humans. Since the entire planet has been unalterably changed by our species—and by other species as well— this edict presents an impossible challenge. Instead we can look at the planet as a network of interrelated relationships that can be mindfully enriched. For more on this idea, see *The Rambunctious Garden* by Emma Marris.

Consider ways in which the land you care for is in relationship with you, and ways you can relate to the plants, animals, stones, and waterways as beings deserving of respect. What do they tell you? What do you tell them?

If you don't already get your eggs from a local, free-range source (like the backyard!), pledge to buy those labeled as certified humane, pasture-fed, or at least free-range for at least one week. What do you notice about their consistency, flavor, and color? Organic, free-range eggs have three times the nutrients as conventional eggs. They are less likely to contain salmonella, which grows in the presence of the stress hormone cortisol.[53] Most people who have made the switch agree that they also just taste better.

# April 14

Save your eggshells for reuse in the garden. Crunch them up and sprinkle onto paths and beds; this deters cats from doing their business in the garden and snails and slugs from eating your plants. Grind them even finer and sprinkle onto tomato plants, who like a lot of calcium. Use half an eggshell as a little seed starter. Rinse out the shell and put it back in the egg carton. Fill with organic potting soil and plant with seeds. When you transplant your seedlings to the garden, gently crack up the shell and plant the whole thing.

# April 15

The Celtic month of Saille, or willow, begins today. Willow lives partly in water and partly on land, like frogs and water fowl. It is of the dreamworld (water) and the land of matter (earth); it forms a bridge between this world and the next. Willow branches poked in wet earth can sprout and grow new roots, and willow bark has a natural compound that will help other plants grow roots as well. Soak willow bark, collected with respect for the tree, in water, then water plant cuttings with this solution to encourage them to grow roots.

Those of us who live an earth- and spirit-centered life are bridges between the mainstream culture and a more ecocentric way of living. If you struggle with this task of bridging worlds, call on willow to help guide and strengthen you. Visit her in meditation and ask for her guidance.

# April 16

Dandelion greens are high in vitamin A, C, potassium, calcium, iron, and B-complex vitamins. They cleanse the blood, tonify the liver, and aid digestion.

Susun Weed offers a tasty recipe in *Healing Wise* for dandelion greens, which are best when they first come up in spring before the flowers appear (though you can eat them anytime). Oriental dandelion soup calls for 5 ounces soba noodles, 8 cups dandelion leaves, 1 cup chopped onion, 2 tablespoons dried kelp, 1 tablespoon grated ginger, ½ cup scallion tops, and 3 tablespoons miso diluted in ½ cup water.

Cook soba noodles and chopped dandelion greens in boiling water 10 minutes. Sauté onions in olive oil; add onions and everything else but the miso to the boiling water. Cook 5–10 minutes. Remove from heat, add diluted miso, and enjoy.[54] Your liver will thank you.

Gardeners and ecologists both are learning that the key to a healthy environment is biodiversity. The web of life is more than the sum of its parts, creating an alchemy beyond simple connections. When planting your garden or helping to plan a community garden or other shared space, include as many species as possible. Include many fruit trees, flowers, grasses, and several native species. Include animals like chickens and bees, and places for wild animals to come enjoy the garden, like a bird bath or sunflowers grown just for the birds. Also consider different heights when planting: tall trees, medium trees, shrubs, flowers, and groundcover, the layering of which creates multiple niches and purposes in the garden.

# April 18

The zone theory of permaculture draws concentric circles around the center of the garden—the house or school—and designates each ring a zone. Zone 1, closest to the house (and along well-traveled paths, and not along any side of the house you rarely visit), is where you put things you access daily, like lettuces, tender herbs, the compost pile, the clothes line, etc. Zone 2, farther from the house, contains things you don't attend daily: dwarf fruit trees, a little pond, a hedge, perennial herbs, and slow-to-mature plants like corn and potatoes. Zone 3 is pasture and large fruit trees, and zone 4 is for growing timber and gathering wild foods; many urban homesteads will not have a zone 3 or 4. Zone 5 is wilderness. Even a small garden should have at least some area dedicated to native plants and space for wildlife.

How can you implement the zone approach to your garden, playground, or home? A simple way is to plant lettuces and herbs just outside the back door, so you can pick them daily and easily reseed when you have room to do so.

# April 19

Add color and springiness to salads with violet flowers. Pick several handfuls and sprinkle atop a salad of spring greens. Freeze into ice cubes and add to iced tea, or candy them to decorate cakes or cupcakes.

To candy flowers, wash gently in cool water and spread to dry on paper towels. Make a sugar syrup by dissolving 1 cup sugar in 1½ cups water heated gently on the stove. Dip violets into the syrup using tweezers, then place on waxed paper. Dust dipped flowers with superfine sugar. Snip off any stems with scissors. Let the sugared flowers dry on waxed paper. When dry, add to cakes or store in an airtight glass container in single layers separated by waxed paper.

## April 20

What has been calling to you in dreams lately? When you begin to work more closely with the land and see the intrinsic value of nature for its own self, the land will begin to talk to you. Your own nature begins to speak more loudly through dreams, omens, and physical symptoms. Take some time today with a cup of herbal tea and your journal to draw images from your dreams. What are they telling you? If messages are not immediately forthcoming, just let them play at the edge of your consciousness and see what arises spontaneously.

# April 21

Today the sun enters the sign of Taurus, which expresses the energies of stability, security, and patience. Venus rules this sign, giving Taureans a love of beauty and luxury. Today would be a good day for a mud bath or a mud mask, reveling in the luxuriant blessings of the earth. Or take some time today to attend to security. In what ways do you feel insecure? Today is a day to organize finances, fix that broken porch step, or refresh any protective wards you have placed on your house. The earth provides us with all our needs. How can you better trust the support of the earth?

To get a larger yield from your garden (whether you have an acre or a window box), practice succession planting. Each week plant a row of radishes, spinach, lettuces, carrots, or beets. They will mature over a longer period of time, extending your harvest.

For plants that mature all at once, like corn or tomatoes, rather than succession planting, plant different varieties that mature at different times. The back of each seed packet will tell you how many days to maturation; mix different growing lengths to get a longer harvest period.

# April 23

Succession planting is a good metaphor for life projects, too. When we plant seeds, sometimes it takes a long time for them to germinate, and we may begin to wonder if they will ever come up at all. When the first seeds germinate, we can wait more patiently for the next week's planting.

Are there projects you began last fall or winter that are just now germinating? How about seeds planted years ago? I wrote my first book, *Sacred Land,* when my daughter was a newborn. She took five or six forty-five-minute naps each day, during which I would write. All these little seeds planted over time added up to a book. Several books over many years slowly mature into a career. Take some time today to write about your own seeds waiting beneath the soil or seedlings at different points of sprouting. Seed germination has a lot to teach us about faith.

## April 24

Our seedlings all need fertilizer, food made from the death and byproducts of other living things. Dead animals make great fertilizer, available in the forms of fish emulsion and blood meal. I buried the placentas from both of my children under fruit trees, organs which came not from death but life. Menstrual blood and urine watered down also make great fertilizers (see May 14). Compost and worm casings from a worm bin also capitalize on the byproducts of decay and consumption.

Consider what died in your life that fertilized your current projects. Create a ritual today that gives thanks to those deaths—relationships, old parts of yourself, jobs—that fueled who you are today.

# April 25

Worm bins are fairly easy to make, and the liquid and solid fertilizers from them are invaluable. A simple worm bin can be made out of two reclaimed dark plastic containers that stack together, like old storage bins. Drill holes in the bottom of one for drainage. Stack them, one inside the other, and drill air holes near the top that go through both containers. Fill the bottom with newspaper and a handful of kitchen waste—peelings, tea bags, too-ripe fruit. Don't use bread, meat, or citrus. Get some worms from a friend with a bin or purchase red worms at a garden center (earth worms from the garden won't be happy in garbage—they need soil). Keep feeding them food scraps, adding paper if it gets too wet, and harvest handfuls of castings to put on your plants. Every now and then lift the inside bin up and pour the liquid fertilizer (worm tea) onto plants or into a spray bottle to spray on the leaves of plants, called a

foliar feed. For more, see *Wiggly Workers* by Diane Cheek
or *Worms Eat My Garbage* by Mary Appelhof, or check
out http://whatcom.wsu.edu/ag/compost/easywormbin
.htm.

# April 26

Write a letter today to your city council and the local paper supporting greening projects, such as allowing urban chickens, permitting front-yard gardens (which are strangely illegal in many cities), or installing solar panels on the city's libraries. Focus on educating and polite requests. Speaking out makes a difference. For more on how to encourage change, see "Engaging Local Government in Transition Work" at http://transitionus .org/event/engaging-local-government-transition-work.

## April 27

Prayer for the day:

Creator, I give thanks for the areas of my life unfolding. I pray for the grace of understanding as I foray into new phases of life. Rebirth comes with pain as well as joy. Help me to witness the pain without suffering. Help me to allow the joy to fill me up to overflowing. Guide me to the teachers I need. Let my gifts and discoveries flow into the world. Help me to help others as they awaken.

# April 28

Another way to fertilize the garden is by growing plants that suck minerals deep from the earth and into their leaves, called nutrient accumulators. When the plant drops leaves or dies in the winter, it provides nutrient-rich mulch that aids its neighbors. Include in your garden comfrey, lamb's quarters, dandelion, and clover. Many weeds are nutrient accumulators. An easy way to use them as fertilizers is to pull them up (preferably before they produce seed heads) and put them through a chipper or go over them with the lawn mower, then use the resulting mulch on your garden beds.

## April 29

Take time today to do nothing. Just sit in the garden or at a favorite park. Spring can be such a busy time as we fertilize, plant, cultivate, write letters, and clean. Take time today to sit outside and ground yourself. Let the earth recharge you. Let your presence simply be in relationship with the land.

# April 30

*"Thou makest springs gush forth in the valleys;*
*they flow between the hills,*
*they give drink to every beast of the field;*
*the wild asses quench their thirst.*
*By them the birds of the air have their habitation;*
*They sing among the branches.*
*From thy lofty abode thou waterest the mountains;*
*The earth is satisfied with the fruit of thy work."*
· · · · · ·
Psalm 104

While this psalm was written in Hebrew and directed at the Hebrew God, it reminds me of a couple of goddesses, Danu and Yemoja. Danu, the mother goddess of Ireland, is the patroness of rivers, water, wells, prosperity, plenty, and wisdom. About Yemoja, worshiped in Nigeria, Haiti, Central America, and Cuba, Burleigh Mutén writes, "As a goddess of fresh springs, she rolls over in her sleep and water gushes out of her round body."[55]

Today, call on God, Yemoja, Danu, and any other water deity you feel connected to. Call to mind the fall-out of climate change and overuse of resources: frequent droughts, melting glaciers and ice caps, drained rivers. Ask that Spirit flow through humanity to restore and rebalance the waters.

# Beltane

At Beltane "the Goddess and God join in love and the earth blossoms in ecstasy."[56] The May Day holiday with paper baskets of flowers and pastel ribbons tied to a pole comes from Beltane. This is a festival of love, flowers, and fairies. It is about passion and creativity and the shift from spring into early summer. It is a fire festival, when Celtic peoples would extinguish their hearth fires (which were usually banked at night but not completely put out), then relight the fire in the morning from the central bonfire lit by the spiritual leader of the community. Fire is about passion and transformation; it is these energies we will play with over the next six weeks. Another important symbol of Beltane is the Green Man, the god of the woods and of green and growing things. We will dance with him and the fey in the literal and spiritual garden, exploring how to grow more, attune with the land, and co-create a bounty we can then share with others.

# May 1

Let yourself have fun today. Dress in flowy clothes in shades of spring-into-summer. Play with the trees, wash your face with dew, and craft a daisy chain or dandelion crown. When we play, we enter into an open space where we can fall in love with nature and spirit. We fill with joy. When filled with love and joy, we open ourselves to transformation. We raise the energy of all around us.

Tonight, light a fire with several different woods, if possible. Traditional sacred woods include apple, hawthorn, birch, alder, oak, holly, and cedar, to name a few. If lighting a bonfire or a smaller fire in an outdoor fire pit isn't possible and you haven't a fireplace, use a charcoal disc in a well-ventilated area, and sprinkle bits of wood into the lit charcoal. Pass ritual items, jewelry, and other noncombustible items through the flame or smoke to purify for the coming year.

# May 2

*Creativity is not about painting a picture or producing an object; it is about wrestling with the demons and angels in the depths of our psyches and daring to name them, to put them where they can breathe and have space and we can look at them.*
Matthew Fox[57]

Today, practice art as meditation—a way to access the Via Creativa, or path to Spirit, through creativity and giving birth. Picture in your mind the big bang, the flaring forth of the universe being birthed. Hold in your hands the fire in your heart, daring to be expressed in the world. Remember or imagine giving birth, the pain of being pulled open from within, followed by the release and joy of holding that new person—hello and welcome, precious one! Then release the energy that flows from within. You can dance, sing, paint, write, cook, garden ... The point is not to make something,

but to co-create with the Goddess. Let it flow. Let it be communion and prayer. Make space in your life for your own flaring forth.

# May 3

*"There is a great deal of talk these days about saving the environment. We must, for the environment sustains our bodies. But as humans we also require support for our spirits, and this is what certain kinds of places provide. The catalyst that converts any physical location— any environment, if you will—into a place is the process of experiencing deeply."*

Alan Gussow[58]

When I taught environmental education, I got to know an area of forest that became alive and very precious and relevant to me. The following year a big section of that forest was clear-cut, and the pain of this loss brought me to my knees. It is for this forest and others like it that I push for environmental stewardship and responsibility.

What places have you experienced deeply? Write about these places and your emotional connection to them. How have these experiences inspired you to action?

# May 4

*"We are homesick for places, we are reminded of places, it is the sounds and smells and sights of places which haunt us and against which we often measure our present."*
••••••
Alan Gussow[59]

To continue from yesterday ... it isn't always possible to visit the places against which we measure our present, places that have become a part of our map of the world and our place in it. We can, however, seek out an emotional experience with the land we now occupy. If you have small children, they can help you with this, as they occupy the space without filters of past experience.

Enter the space you occupy, whether you live in a house with a yard, a condo with a common garden space, or a patch of city land whose connection with unpaved spaces includes only a few sidewalk trees or an abandoned lot. Ground yourself by feeling your feet on the land and your energy sinking into the earth below you. Ask the space to reveal itself to you. Walk around, slowly, taking in your senses until something catches your attention. Sit with this thing: a bird's nest, a curl of tasseled grass, a stone—it doesn't matter what it is. Sit with it. Talk to it, and let it talk to you. Allow it to enter you deeply. Let yourself play.

# May 5

As we transition from spring toward summer, reflect back on the past several months. We've transitioned from the water of winter to the wood of spring. You've hatched from an egg, planted seeds, and examined where you are unfolding, germinating, and rooting.

Spring is about the Via Creativa and art as meditation. What projects have rooted, sprouted, and flowered as you move toward making fruit? How is your dance with fire—passion and release—playing out? How can you continue to align yourself with these energies? Write and meditate on your journey.

# May 6

A useful tool when planning and caring for your garden is muscle testing. If you have ever seen applied kinesiology, you have experienced this tool for tapping into the subconscious mind and the energy fields surrounding the body. When something is true, the electric impulses in our muscles fire; when something is not true or doesn't serve us, the electric field is weakened and so are our muscles.

While this technique has been criticized as unscientific quackery, I have found it to be very useful when checking in with both my body and the garden. To use it in the garden, make an O-shape out of your thumb and forefinger. Do the same with the other hand, then interlock the two circles. Tug firmly on the little chain shape, not letting the circles break. State something true, such as "My name is [your name]," and tug. Now

state something false: "My name is Asparagus," and tug—your fingers will not be able to hold the chain.

This works whether you know the answer or not, as it is based on the integrity of the energy fields in and around your body. I used this recently with the compost: "I should turn the compost" elicited a broken grasp, while "I should leave the compost to sit" resulted in a strong grasp. I left the pile to cook on its own. I tried this technique with some anemic-looking strawberry plants that didn't seem to respond to water or compost and determined they needed fish fertilizer. They perked up and looked greener the very next day. Give it a try in your garden.

In addition to muscle testing and planting date charts, use your gut to determine what the garden needs. Ask a question or make a statement, such as "Should I plant a pear tree here?" and then pay attention to your stomach. A tight or slightly anxious feeling there indicates no, while a relaxed, uplifted feeling indicates yes. Whether this is your unconscious mind communicating to you based on all the information it has picked up and processed without the conscious mind's awareness, or it is attunement with the field of the tree, the land, and the garden devas, it works. The trick is to be able to calm your own mind enough to trust your gut. Use this tool in other areas of life as well.

# May 8

A traditional practice at Beltane is to wish on a haw-thorn tree. Many sacred wells around the world also have a sacred tree associated with them, and many people wish or pray for healing by tying a little strip of cloth onto the branches of this sacred tree. To make such a wish, use a little strip of natural cloth. Mentally send your wishes for health, prosperity, or other change into the cloth. Find a sacred tree—any tree that calls to you—and tell it your wish. Tie the strip to a branch and give the tree thanks.

The cloth is a symbol of our intention, and the tree, with its great arms reaching to the sky and its mas-sive roots stretching into the Underworld, is a bridge between all worlds, helping us to manifest our most enlightened life.

# May 9

What do you wish for most of all? What ignites your passion? When we know and honor our passions, we truly live, and we help others to do the same. Write about what makes you passionately alive. What are your core images or dreams? In what ways are you living these passions?

If you don't really know what your passions are or how to live them more fully, try making a dream collage, or what a music therapist friend of mine calls her "treasure map." Look through magazines or online for images that pull on your heart. Glue them onto a piece of thick paper or cardboard. Decorate the collage with glitter, if you like—have fun! Hang your treasure map where you can see it every day. It may take a while—years even—but with this map you will find your way, igniting passions in your job, hobbies, and personal life.

# May 10

Civilized Western culture tends to be afraid of passion and strong emotions. We feel uncomfortable crying in front of others, being too exuberant, or expressing rage. Sexual passion has been co-opted by movie stars and pornography. These fears come from a fear of the body—the vessel of emotion—and of the ecstasy of Spirit.

In your journal, write about memories of when your passion as a child or teen was stifled in some way. This may have been something another person said or a situation where you held yourself back. See how your responses to these moments or situations were motivated by your need to survive. We need to be accepted by others, and we need to be physically and emotionally safe. Sometimes this means dampening our passions.

Send compassion to these parts of yourself that feared being expressed or that still fear living a passionate life. Light a candle and see the flame as God's love filling you with compassion.

When have you encountered the ecstasy of Spirit? These are the moments, often unexpected, when you are brought to your knees, tears spilling over, filled with laughter and love. We encounter the Goddess in nature, while in prayer or meditation, talking with a loved one, at births and deaths, and in random moments of grace. Write or paint about these moments, or share them with another person. How do you feel when you revisit them? What does it inspire in you?

# May 12

Many people in our fast-paced society rarely go outside, except from the house to the car, the car to the store, the store to work or school, and back to the house. If you've been to a park recently, have you noticed how many adults are staring at smartphones instead of the trees or clouds? Outside becomes something we pass through. In our modern culture, if you garden, hike, camp, or just play outside, you are in the minority.

Think about how you might help others get outside. You might:

> · start a garden program at a local school
>
> · volunteer to walk in the park with house-bound senior citizens
>
> · have business meetings outside in the courtyard once a month (or more)
>
> · organize a block-party barbecue to get people into their front yards

- start or participate in a garden therapy program at a botanic garden, local farm, or community garden (see the American Horticultural Therapy Program's website at www.ahta.org)

# May 13

Today begins the Celtic month of Huath, or hawthorn. Along with oak and ash, the hawthorn is said to be one of the three trees through which we can access the fairy realm. It is associated with chastity, which is related to the pure of heart and childlike open-mindedness, qualities needed to access the fey (though not necessarily chastity itself). Hawthorn's flowering marks the beginning of the light half of the year, but the lovely flowers and foliage mask a sharp thorn. Hawthorn represents beauty and light, but also caution.

As we have seen with the Via Negativa and the Via Positiva, both polarities are a part of spiritual living. Do you tend to overemphasize either New Age sparkly light or doomsday environmental darkness? Meditate or journal on the pure white flowers and the long, sharp thorns of hawthorn. In what ways can these energies help you find balance in your life?

## May 14

I mentioned it way back in November, and it probably grossed you out a little—but I'm going to mention it again. Urine, watered down 20 parts water to 1 part urine, makes a great fertilizer. It's high in nitrogen and contains trace minerals. It can also contain bacteria, so if you are ill or taking any medications, skip this tip. But if you are healthy, feed your tomato seedlings and leafy greens with fertilizer from your very own kidneys. Tomatoes can handle it slightly less watered down, because a little salt makes them stronger (if you have access to sea water, use that as fertilizer every now and then on your tomatoes). It also deters squirrels from the garden. Once I started using it liberally, the marauders stopped digging in my beds.

# May 15

Prayer for today:

Goddess, help me to face my passions with courage. I know that my life's calling will help make the planet a better place for all. Guide me as I seek to live my soul's passion every day in ways big and small. Living my truth in this world can sometimes be frightening and lonely work. Help me to find the right community, teachers, and place in the world to live fully, in service to life. Thank you.

# May 16

*“We are utterly dependent on plants. We wake up in houses made of wood from the forests of Maine, pour a cup of coffee brewed from coffee beans grown in Brazil, throw on a T-shirt made of Egyptian cotton, print out a report on paper, and drive our kids to school in cars with tires made of rubber that was grown in Africa and fueled by gasoline derived from cycads that died millions of years ago.”*

Daniel Chamovitz[60]

Make it a game today to notice how you depend on plants. What examples besides Chamovitz's list do you encounter? Say them to yourself as you notice them throughout your day.

# May 17

One of the ways we are combining the creativity of nature with modern technology to change our species' relationship with the earth is through biomimicry, which draws from natural design in plants, animals, waterways, and other natural designs to engineer the human world. Examples include wind turbines designed like humpback whale flippers to increase their efficiency, high-rise air-conditioning systems based on self-cooling termite mounds, and carbon dioxide sequestering systems designed like human lungs.

Simpler examples of biomimicry include compost piles, water-filtration pitchers, and even your shower head. Where can you find nature's design principles in your daily life? For more inspiring examples, visit websites like AskNature.org and Earthsky.org.

## May 18

Create a sacred space outdoors, a place for reflection and communion. This might be a labyrinth crafted out of stones or mowed into tall grass, a shrine out of an old bathtub or crate, or a corner garden dedicated to a loved one who has crossed over. Include crystals and stones, a statue of a favorite goddess, plants or flowers, and a place to sit. Water marks many of our sacred places; if you haven't a pond or a view of the ocean, a simple bird bath or fountain will do just fine. A pretty pot or bowl and an inexpensive pump can transform any garden corner into a sacred altar. Bless your space by sprinkling it with salt and burning a little incense (carefully, of course), then sit in silence and let the space speak to you.

# May 19

Make some simple goddess figurines or images of leaves and flowers out of air-hardening clay, available at craft stores. One simple way to do this is to roll a ball of clay about the size of a marble, then press it flat into your palm. Then take a button or stamp that has a flower, fairy, or spiral design on it and press it into the clay. Or mold the clay into any shape, like a Venus of Willendorf goddess. Make a dozen or so, then let them dry.

Carry your little figurines with you wherever you go, and leave them as blessings wherever you feel called to do so. Maybe there is a tree outside your office who greets you each day; leave it a token of gratitude and blessing. Perhaps you see a flower growing unexpectedly in the grass strip next to a gas station; give it a blessings and thanks. Or when you come across a person who could use a little magic, press the little goddess into her palm with a smile.

If you have room for a fruit tree on your property, use the following technique to improve the soil and reuse what might otherwise be considered waste. On a hill (slight or steep), dig a trench about halfway down the slope, perpendicular to the slope. This is called a swale. Downhill from the trench, peel off or dig up any sod in an area about five feet in diameter for each tree. On top of this soil, next to the trench, mound branches and rotting logs about a foot high. Take the chunks of sod you dug up, and lay them grass-side-down onto the brush pile. This is called a German mound, or *hugelkultur* bed. Cover this pile with the soil from the trench, then plant a fruit tree or other plants on this mound. If you like, fill the swale with brush or straw. The swale catches rainwater as it pours down the hill, then slowly releases it into the mound and the fruit tree's roots. The decaying brush beneath the tree decays slowly, releasing nitrogen and heat while improving the soil.

# May 21

Another easy way to improve soil is to create a trench composter. Dig a trench anywhere you want to improve the soil, keeping the dirt alongside your ditch. Fill with grass clippings, kitchen waste, and other things you might throw in a composter. Since this will be buried right away, you can even include bones from last night's dinner (after you make stock!). As you put organic matter into the trench, cover it with the soil you dug out to protect it from critters. You can plant this pile with seeds or seedlings, or let it sit and compost in place until you're ready to plant.

# May 22

Today the sun enters Gemini, the sign of the heavenly twins. Gemini is a mutable air sign, which means it comes between spring and summer, is flexible, and is focused on the mind and communication. Imagine a butterfly dancing from one blossom to the next. As she lands, her twin wings open and close.

In what ways do you feel split in two? In what areas are you "two-faced"? Duality can be balancing, as in day and night, or it can indicate incompletion or something needing more attention, as in a quiet adder that suddenly lashes out. In meditation, imagine you are a butterfly or a snake. What do these forms bring out in you? Journal or create art about your meditation.

# May 23

The passionate self is at home in nature. She is comfortable with her sexuality. She loves to dance, sing, drum, live. Go outside today with a drum. Close your eyes; ground your energy. Let a natural heartbeat rhythm arise from deep within the earth. Feel the Mother's heartbeat. Now drum that rhythm. Beat your drum to the rhythm of the earth. Let it move you. Let it awaken you. Drum as long as you like, letting her heartbeat fill your body and soul. When the drumming naturally releases you, place your hands and forehead on the earth to return to your body.

# May 24

When you feel the passion of anger, sadness, joy, ecstasy, or some other possibly overwhelming emotion, notice where it exists in your body. What happens on a somatic level when those emotions arise? The "e" in emotion is energy. An emotion is the motion of energy. To stop its movement in our bodies—to quickly turn it off or divert it—is to stunt our own growth just as a tree would be stunted when cut off from the sun's energy. To let that energy explode unchecked into externalized behaviors like violence is like letting an invasive weed take over a garden. Seek balance and health by fully experiencing the somatic part of the emotion, owning it as your experience and letting it speak to you. It will provide clarity from which you can take action. When the human race can experience and own our passions, we will be able to live in harmony with the earth. We will no longer seek to dominate matter—the land, women, etc.—but will be able to flow with matter like a tree growing strong in its right place.

BELTANE

## May 25

To ignite the fires of love, make an Aphrodite oil by mixing 4 tablespoons almond oil with 3–5 drops each rose oil, (synthetic) musk oil, and ambergris oil, then add a pinch of ground cinnamon. Store in a lovely bottle in a sacred place, then wear your oil for passion and to draw love to you. Create a ritual in which you pledge yourself to your creative spirit and the goddess who is your muse.[61] Include as a part of your ritual a dedication to loving yourself better. Rub Aphrodite oil on your stomach or chest, feel pinkish-golden light surrounding you, and let it infuse your heart center. Repeat the phrase "I am love." Let whatever comes arise and be experienced. Dance with Aphrodite, Brigid, Nefertiti, and Freya. Send your love deep into the earth. Your love will attract love to you.

# May 26

Bees are creatures of air, but at this fiery time of year they teach us about love and passion. They are little fertility goddesses. Besides the sacred honeybee, our bee friends include bumblebees, mason bees, and leaf-cutter bees. Protect bees by never using pesticides and by eating and growing organic. Attract bees to your garden with flowers from fruit trees, bee balm, dandelions, clover, and other flowering plants. You may be interested in learning to keep honeybees (ask local farmers or see www.bee culture.com), or in attracting mason bees and bumblebees to your yard by providing them with their own houses, which require almost no maintenance. See February 21 for more on mason bee and bumblebee houses.

# May 27

If you want a garden but have no space, or if you want to extend the growing area you already have, put a garden on the side of your house or garage, literally on the wall. Buy some 8-foot PVC white rain gutter and drill holes in the bottom every inch or so with a ⅛-inch drill bit. Cap the ends with PVC gutter end caps. Bolt the gutter planter to an open wall or hang it from a pergola with ⅛-inch diameter steel cables. You could also use reclaimed gutters as long as they haven't been painted with toxic house paint. Fill with organic potting soil and plant with greens, herbs, strawberries, baby carrots, or pansies. For pictures and more detailed instructions, search "hanging gutter garden" and "wall gutter garden" online.

## May 28

Can you make watering more efficient in your yard and garden? Put a bucket in your shower to catch gray water, then pour the captured water on your flower beds and at the base of fruit trees. After washing vegetables in a bowl of water, pour that back in the garden. Wash plastic milk or juice jugs in warm, soapy water, cut off the bottom of the jugs, and bury them upside down next to water-hungry plants like tomatoes and pumpkins. Fill the jug when you water; the water will seep slowly into the roots. Set up a rain barrel to catch runoff from your garage or house, and use the captured water to irrigate the garden or lawn.

# May 29

Go outside naked. Whether you slip into the backyard under the cloak of darkness, go skinny dipping, or take a sun-heated shower while backwoods camping, figure out a way to get outside with no clothes on. Feeling wind, water, sunlight, and soil on parts of you usually covered up deepens your relationship with the earth in surprising ways. Besides the sensory experience, the sense of vulnerability creates an intimacy with the natural world.

One thing that stops us from being our passionate selves is shame. Shame is also responsible for our subjugation of others, including our subjugation of the earth. When we are at peace with ourselves, we can stand as equals with others, no matter their sexual orientation, religion, or species.

The healing of shame can be a long, painful process. Prayer, compassion toward the self, therapy, and ritual can all help heal shame. Write down on little pieces of paper whatever you are ashamed of in yourself. These are the things that arose as you journaled about limitations upon your passion. They are the images in your nightmares. They are the issues we get mad at others for bringing up. If you can't name them, just draw symbols or images that arise as you consider them.

Burn these pieces of paper (be safe with the fire, of course), ritually letting go of the things that bind you. Ask for the grace of wisdom and healing.

# May 31

Go outside and stand barefoot on the earth. If you can put your feet in water or damp earth, even better. When we stand, sit, or lie in direct contact with the earth, electrons from the planet flow freely through our bodies, equalizing EMFs and other electrical charges in the body. Studies by the Earthing Institute, which have largely been ignored by Western science possibly because they are so basic and simple, found that grounding yourself by standing on the earth reduces inflammation (the cause of most chronic illness today), improves sleep, reduces pain, reduces jet lag, and decreases unwanted symptoms of PMS and menopause. See www .earthing.net.

# June 1

Go camping! Whether you stay in a tent or prefer to rent a cabin or a yurt, get yourself and your family or some friends (or take a personal retreat) out into the natural world. You may have to reserve a campsite now for next year, or you can call now and find out if there are any cancellations or openings. Many parks and private campsites have accessible trails and ramps. If you are able, try hiking a short (or longer) distance to a campsite farther from the whir of airplanes and the buzz of cell phones. A minimum of two nights is ideal— it takes at least that long for the tension of modern life to melt from our bodies—but even one night away can rejuvenate our connection with the uncivilized land. Try reserveamerica.com in the US or search a nearby city plus "camping," or ask friends for a recommendation of where to go.

# June 2

The Earth's iron core produces the planet's electromagnetic field, making Earth a giant electromagnetic battery. This field gives us north and south poles. It is the field animals follow when migrating. It also protects us from the sun's solar wind, which "blows" the field away on the far side of the earth. When drawn, the depiction of the earth's magnetic field looks like a giant angel surrounding the earth, with our home planet at the angel's throat (to see a depiction of the earth's magnetic field blown by the sun, see http://www.teara.govt.nz/en/atmosphere/1/5).Could part of our reason for existence on earth be to learn to communicate, which is the energy of the throat chakra? Meditate on the throat chakra today, focusing your energy on your center of communication. When you focus on this area, what comes up for you? Allow any emotion to flow. Record any images or thoughts that arise in your journal.

# June 3

A Native American name for June is Strawberry Moon.[62] The contemporary Druid name for this time of year is Field Poppy Moon.[63] Both are images of bright red against vibrant green. The perfect June sundress, in my mind, would be in a strawberry print. June is a time to set back and feel the pulse of the summer before it gets too hot. It's a time to gently consider your place in the web of life. Picture in your mind yourself tied to your family members, friends, and community members, like strawberry plants tied by runners. How do you support each other? What is your role?

# June 4

> *Earth voices are glad voices, and the Earth-songs come up from the ground through the plants; and in their flowering, and in the days before these days are come, they do tell Earth songs to the wind.*
>
> Opal Whiteley, age 6 [64]

My daughter, also six, sometimes sings a rambling, humming, wandering sort of warble as she plays or cooks or meanders outside. After spending several hours in the garden or hiking or at the beach doing nothing but being and exploring and listening, you may begin to feel a sort of Earth song not unlike my daughter's warbling. Your body slips into a time-out-of-time phase. You can sense the Earth song rising from the plants and their flowering. Try it—give yourself at least three hours to just be in nature with no agenda. Let the music of the land arise around and within you.

# June 5

A tip from a friend of mine:

> I've been having my morning coffee out on my back porch. Previously, I would have it in front of the computer while checking email or browsing Facebook, but this morning I was struck by all there was to see. Birds in and out of the tree, a bee collecting pollen from my drooping sunflower, squirrels calling to each other and racing along the power lines, gorgeous clouds nearly covering the deep blue end-of-summer sky. There was so much movement and so much noise ...
>
> I noticed as I came in this morning that there was a small smile on my face rather than a furrow on my brow. I hope to carry the peace with me through the day. And now

I want to tell everyone, "Just go sit outside! Do you know what's out there? It's amazing!" But then I think ... it seems to be the kind of thing, perhaps like faith, that you just can't force upon another. You can live it and revel in it and be available when someone comes along and says "what's the fuss all about?" But you just can't force a person to be amazed by the chaotic dance of some unidentified insects in the rising sun.

... And if you haven't already put it in your book, one of your days should be "have your morning coffee outside."[65]

# June 6

Form a group with friends and neighbors to go explore local natural areas. Grab the kids, pack up a lunch, and head out on a regular basis to a trail, a green space, or a body of water just to play and learn by being in a natural habitat as a group. Going as a group

- can reduce fear, as there is safety in numbers
- can be created and joined by any kind of family
- creates motivation to just get out and do it
- provides an opportunity to share knowledge
- and can cost very little to nothing[66]

## June 7

Lie on the ground and look up. Passing over you on a clear summer day are between three and six billion insects traveling along in a "bug highway" of wind currents. Close to the equator, on warm, balmy days, will be even more bugs, while over the UK, scientist Jason Chapman counted close to three billion insects zipping about as far as 19,000 feet high. Most are between 2,000 and 5,000 feet high, looking for food, mates, or just more space.[67]

What would it be like to soar above the earth as an insect? To fly from tree to tree, passing mountains, buzzing and passing frass (aka bug poop) and clicking and laying eggs? Imagine yourself as an insect. What kind of bug would you be? Where would you go? What would you do?

# June 8

To learn more about the plants local to your area, go on a weed walk. You can either check out a book on native plants and weeds from the library and go exploring yourself or find a local guide. Herb shops, botanic gardens, and natural history museums often offer such tours. If you cannot find one already set up, contact a local herbalist or botanist (try a local university) and ask her or him to put something together for your family or a group. Learning what grows around you, especially the weeds tucked in the corners and the edible plants, will bring your home ecology alive.

# June 9

*"The heavens are telling the glory of God; and the firmament proclaims his handiwork."*
· · · · · ·
Psalm 19

Consider this psalm today as you stare at clouds, experience today's weather, and notice the changing colors of the sky. All of nature proclaims the handiwork of the Divine. Take some time to stare at the sky, and meditate or journal on the glory of the firmament.

# June 10

The Celtic month of Duir begins today, named for the oak, tree of strength, honor, and male virility. Oak is strong and straight. Oaks live for hundreds of years, growing gnarled and wise. Oak teaches us about patience and steadfastness. The acorn, oak trees' seed, is a symbol of hope, nourishment, and the future.

June is often a time of endings: the end of school, spring weather, and for some the fiscal year; but it is also a time of beginnings: summer vacation, travel, and the bounty of summer gardens and farmers' markets. It is a masculine time of year, when we move into the fire and yang energies of the summer months. As we near the summer solstice, meditate on your own strength. Imagine yourself an oak reaching high into the sky and deep into the earth. Or sit at the base of an oak and ask that it lend you strength and virility.

# June 11

Designate an area of the garden to grow more food than your family can eat, and grow extra for local food pantries, your child's (or niece's or neighbor kids') classroom, or the elderly neighbor next door. Plants that grow a lot of produce include zucchini, cucumber, fruit trees, and orach. Your climate may be really fabulous at growing something else, too—plant some of whatever that is. Community is going to be the key to surviving the changes already affecting our planet due to climate change. Educating others on how to grow fresh food goes a long way toward creating healthy kids and community. For more information on sharing with food pantries, call the Plant A Row foundation at 1-877-492-2727 or see AmpleHarvest.org.

## June 12

A valuable and sometimes overlooked connection with the natural world comes through our pets. "Scientists have found ... that levels of neurochemicals and hormones associated with social bonding are elevated during animal-human interactions."[68] Pets help root us to the world of social interaction while giving us a kiss of the wild. Caring for pets reminds us of basic daily needs: food, water, shelter, love. We have all heard stories of pets knowing when we are ill or sad, and of the deep bonds they form with us. Pets teach children about compassion and care. Spend some time with your pets today, witnessing them and being with them without racing off to some important human activity. If you don't have any pets, consider adopting one that works for you and your family.

## June 13

Go outside early in the morning or at dusk. Your back-yard is fine, or a park or a hike in the woods. Close your eyes and smell. Breathe in deeply. Do different areas smell different? Can you smell water? Rain? Pine trees? Flowers? A friend of mine smelled dragonflies when they flew near her face; she described the smell as musky, heady, salty, and a little mildewy. Some smells we find unpleasant, like dead animals or dog droppings. Others might be unpleasant to others but cherished by you. I love the smell of the fish at Seattle's Pike Place Market and of low tide at the beach. Some smells are hard to explain to someone else: here in Colorado, when the dry summer wind blows warm, it creates a smell on my skin that I love. It's sort of grassy, nutty, and dry.

Dusk and morning aren't crucial times for this exercise, of course, but I find outdoor smells to be partic-ularly sweet at these transition times. What do you notice?

# June 14

Find a spot where you can sit on the earth. You might want to be alone for this one, especially if you have any fears or self-consciousness about singing. Sit for a moment, feeling the space around you. Now relax your throat as much as you can and allow a sound to arise—*aaaaah*—or whatever your voice does. You aren't trying to sing or sound pretty, you're just toning, sort of like an infant trying its voice for the first time. Play with the pitch—how high or low the sound is—to find the most comfortable spot for your voice. Keep relaxing your throat.

When you find your tone, *aaaaah* it (or whatever sound you are making) a while, letting it vibrate you. Now direct that sound down into the earth. Let your voice be a gift to the land. If you feel drawn to, sing it to trees and stones and the water as well.

# June 15

In your journal, write about a place you remember—some place in nature that you long for or that comes up in dreams. Write your sense memories of that place: what did you see, smell, hear, feel, taste? Who was there? What were you doing, and where did you go afterwards?

Now go back to what you have written, and circle phrases that jump out at you—images that really capture the experience of the essence of that place. Assemble the phrases together into a poem. If you like, go back and edit for clarity and flow. Share your poem of place with someone else.

# June 16

*"There's a conversation that keeps going beyond the human level, in many ways, beyond language, extending into the atmosphere itself. Weather is a form of communication."*

● ● ● ● ● ●

Stanley Kunitz[69]

The weather communicates to us humans the state of the earth, the seasons, and upcoming weather; it's a communication we can become aware of by listening and feeling. Step outside in the morning and sense what is coming. How does it affect your mood? Your plans?

The land and sky and water all communicate through weather as well. This communication often happens beyond our human awareness. The land speaks and listens. Trees translate for the earth what the sky is saying. Rain falls and speaks of the far-off ocean. Fog sings to the trees and ferns of monsoons over the Indian Ocean. How much of this can you hear? Eavesdrop on the chatting of the sky and the land.

# June 17

Here in the Denver area, summer nights are punctuated by the chirping of crickets. I like to go outside and sit, close my eyes, and listen deeply to their chorus. The small chartreuse tree crickets and the hefty black field crickets together create a cathedral of sound. I listen to the interweaving of individual chirping as well as the waves of song all across the city. The singing rises and falls until it enters me, turning me into sound. The chirping chorus creates a trance state.

I try to hear what it sounds like if you slow down the song. When a recording of crickets chirping is slowed down several times, it creates what sounds like an angelic chorus. Search "God's cricket chorus" online to hear a sample.

What else sings praise to the universe that we simply take for granted? Listen to the frogs, the birds, the wind. Can you hear the song?

# June 18

The bright light of the sun is expressed within ourselves as our soul purpose. So many people try to figure out what that life purpose is, but it doesn't *need* to be figured out—just allowed to reveal itself to you, much like the sun is revealed after a storm.

Find a time and place where you will not be disturbed. Sit comfortably, breathe, and ground your energy by sinking it into the earth. Cast a circle around you if you like. Now follow your breath in and out, just observing without trying to change your breathing in any way. Notice the deepest place your breath settles in your torso. As you observe, it may settle deeper into your center. With your inner eye, take a look at this deep spot. What do you see? What do you feel?

From this place deep inside you, allow words or images to arise spontaneously. Try not to think too much about them. Let them surface like bubbles from the bottom of a pond. See how these words or images play out in your waking life and in your dreams.

## June 19

Summer is about expansion, growth, outward activity, and creativity. Chinese medicine suggests that we rise early and reach to the sun for nourishment. Eat brightly colored summer fruits and vegetables. Cook with high heat for a short time, and add some spicy and pungent flavors to attune with the yang quality of summer. Apples, watermelon, lemons, and limes help to cool the body. Spice helps to disperse heat, as do hot liquids like chamomile tea. Make a salad or stir-fry with as many colored vegetables as possible, and toss with a little hot sauce for some summer zing.

# Litha

Litha, or midsummer, is the summer solstice, when the hours of light are at their greatest and the sun the farthest north in the sky. It is the opposite of Yule, when the sun is "reborn" after the longest night. This is the longest day, when energy is at its most yang, intense and masculine. Throughout most of the hemisphere, frost dates are long past. The garden grows warm- season fruits. Herbs' leaves radiate power, for most have not yet sent energy into flowering. Insects and birds zip, buzz, and chirp with the glory of the transformation of spring into summer. The exact date of the solstice can vary from June 20–22 in the Northern Hemisphere and December 20–22 in the Southern Hemisphere.

# June 20

This is the best time of year to gather the leaves of herbs, as the plant's energy is focused on making food and has not yet been directed into making flowers or seeds. Culinary herbs like oregano, thyme, sage, and rosemary, and medicinal herbs like comfrey, nettle, and lemon balm, are all herbs whose leaves we use. If you grow herbs in your garden, gather some today with the intention of retaining the sun's great power.

Make a tea out of locally gathered herbs. A mint base, something medicinal, and a pinch of something bitter and cleansing and with a dash of local honey will create a sunny tea for attuning to the power of the solstice. Depending on the weather, you may want this warm, iced, or even poured into ice trays or Popsicle molds. Kids will enjoy rejuvenating Popsicles made from lemon balm and chamomile tea. As you sip or lick your summer treat, meditate on the power of photosynthesis to bring the sun's power to earth and to all of life.

# June 21

Honey is often called liquid gold or liquid sunshine. Hold a bottle up to the sun and see the rays of summer power infuse the transformed nectar into God's light. Hold a jar of honey or a bit of honeycomb in your hand. Close your eyes and direct your awareness into the honey. What do you see? How does it feel in your body? Taste the honey, letting it slowly roll around on your tongue.

A teaspoon of honey is the life's work of twelve bees. They gather nectar—a gift from the flower—and pollen, return to the hive, regurgitate the nectar from their honey stomach, mix it with enzymes, and store it in hexagonal vessels. Then other bees fan it to evaporate much of the water. When they reach just the right amount of moisture, they cap each little cell with wax. Bees eat pollen for protein and honey for carbohydrates. A hive usually produces much more honey than it will need

to get through a winter; we collect the extra. If you are blessed to live near a wild bees' nest, beekeeper's hives, or even a farmers' market offering local honey, make a pilgrimage to this site. Take a moment to pay homage to the bees for their sacred dance and power-filled gift.

The sun enters the astrological sign of Cancer on June 22. Emotionality and intuition can run high. Animals with shells, such as the crab, are associated with this sign and illustrate the energy of Cancer, the soft inside that is carefully protected. Write in your journal about how you express the energy of the crab at this time. Do you need to shore up your protection, or is your shell too thick? Do you feel like hiding under a rock or hunting for nourishment? Have an imaginary conversation with yourself as a crab. What messages does this aspect of yourself offer?

# June 23

When you eat a plant or an animal, you are eating a piece of the big bang. Everything was created in that explosion. Over billions of years these elements danced—birthing, dying, birthing, dying—until a supernova exploded to form the sun, the planets, and all the elements on Earth. Early bacteria mutated photosynthetic processes, which eventually created plants, able to transform light from the sun into food energy. When a plant is consumed, energy transforms again into other forms of life. It is all a great spiral dance. Take a moment while enjoying your summer salad to meditate on this cosmological transformation.

## June 24

Though undetected by our human sensibilities, the days have begun to shorten. Each day the sun will rise a little farther south, though in many climates the heat has just begun. Summer is a juxtaposition of shortening days and pulsing heat. Choose one moment each day at the same time and notice where the sun is in relation to a landmark like a tree, rock promontory, or even a building. You may even want to record this in your journal as it changes throughout the season or year. If you have children, they can outline the shadow of some object with chalk in the same place at the same time each day to see how it moves.

Write a poem today about what you feel slipping away in your life as the sun slips quietly toward the south.

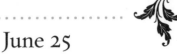

# June 25

Call in a midsummer night's dream. Before you go to bed, write out any questions you have for your guides. Do you wonder about your next steps in life? About the teaching of an illness you are struggling with? Or perhaps you need guidance for a relationship in your life. Ask that they offer guidance through your dreams.

In the morning, before getting out of bed, write down your dreams. Pay attention to the emotional charge in the dream. Write down any images that stand out. Explore how each of the people or animals in the dream is an aspect of yourself. What is the dream saying?

If nothing comes the first night, keep asking, paying attention, and journaling. When you open to the wisdom of dreamtime, magical dreams will come. Pay attention to synchronicities and symbols that arise, like animals appearing in your yard or on walks. The Goddess speaks to us through dreams, nature, and coincidences.

Craft garden markers out of wide, flat stones by painting on them with green and white acrylic paint. First pencil your words or pictures onto your rock, then paint using a fine-tipped acrylic paintbrush. After the paint is completely dry (a few hours to a day), use a foam brush to cover the design with clear waterproof sealer. Let dry. These could be plant labels for herbs, perennials, or vegetables, or you might write sayings like *Faerie Garden* or mark the four directions.[70]

Before placing the stones in the garden, take a moment to hold them in your hands. Close your eyes and infuse the stones with blessings for the plants. Send a message to the plant devas by stating aloud or in your mind your intention for your garden and each plant, then sending that message into the stones.

## June 27

Many climates are quite warm a week past midsummer. Some people live for hot weather, while others feel overstimulated by extreme heat. As our planet warms via climate change, we are feeling the transformative power of fire energy. There are two useful approaches to global warming: cutting greenhouse gas emission and redesigning how we live in response to Earth's changes. An example of how design can change our relationship with the land is amphibious housing in areas prone to flooding and tsunamis, like Bangladesh. These houses are made of light materials like bamboo and recycled plastic bottles, so they can float. They run on solar power, have composting toilets, and capture and recycle rainwater.[71] They can rest on land or float when the land is flooded.

Do three things today that contribute to living in harmony with climate change. This might be hanging out the laundry to dry, riding your bike instead of driving, or researching solar panels for your home. You probably already do many of these things anyway; today, as you make these choices, hold in mind how they connect you to the greater earth and the transforming human community. It can feel lonely making environmentally conscious decisions in a self-absorbed society. Think global and know you are a part of a powerful movement.

# June 28

One way to drastically reduce your carbon footprint is to install solar panels on your house. Until recently, such a change has been unaffordable for most people. Solar-power companies have recently created leasing programs that make it possible for the average homeowner to install solar panels, reducing energy bills and the detrimental effects of coal, nuclear, and hydroelectric power. Most programs offer zero-down leasing programs with options to reduce payments over the life of the system with a small down payment. If you own your home or know someone who does, take a serious look into the possibility of installing solar panels. Ask friends for referrals, look around your neighborhood for yard signs in front of paneled houses, or search online using the keywords "solar panel leasing." Also see *Solar Panel Leasing Review and Company Comparison* at http://solarpowerauthority.com /solar-panel-leasing-review-company-comparison/.

In many cultures, the sun is associated with a god and is regarded as a masculine energy. Mainstream culture has a conflicted relationship with masculine energy, regarding it as the foundation for everything while simultaneously stifling and fearing it. Unhealthy masculine energy is responsible for the rape of the earth. Healthy masculinity is about standing up for oneself and one's values, defining clear boundaries, and protecting one's family. In order to create an ecocentric culture, we all must be able to access and express both healthy masculine and feminine energies.

Do a ritual today for your inner god. Regardless of your gender, call on your healthy masculine side. Envision yourself facing the sun, then stepping into its fire and becoming the sun god. A huge amount of energy will flow through you. Breathe with it. Notice what arises. You might identify areas in your life needing

better-defined boundaries or areas where you are too aggressive and need to step back a little. When you return to your body, take time to ground, and let any excess energy flow into the feminine earth, which will help bring balance. Journal about your ritual.

# June 30

When heat and fire become too yang, we often turn to water to cool us. Interestingly, the formation of water—hydrogen and oxygen combining—produces a large amount of energy, part of which is heat. Water can also hold a huge amount of heat before changing states, so on our watery planet we have lots of ice, liquid water in a wide range of temperatures, and steam.

Today, take a soak in water: a pool, bathtub, hot springs, lake—whatever is available. Notice the heat exchange between you and the water as it cools or warms you. You in turn cool or warm it as well. All of life is about the exchange of energy. Consider this as you go about your day: where else do you exchange energy with the world around you?

# July 1

Light a candle and sit before it. Breathe, ground, and center. Stare into the flame, a piece of the sun transformed. Wax formed by bees or plants, a cotton wick grown from green photosynthesizers, and the combustion of sulfur, phosphorus, and oxygen—all elements formed at the birth of the solar system—unite in this moment to burn a small flame.

Close your eyes and see this flame inside yourself. You, too, consist of elements formed in the supernova that created the solar system. Inside of you, trillions of mitochondria break down organic compounds using oxygen and release energy, just as in a candle flame (though the process and compounds are a little different). Combustion destroys, and it leads to life, and it occurs constantly in and around us.

# July 2

Smudge your house and altar today, drawing on the power of fire and smoke to cleanse. Make your own smudge stick using dried sage, rosemary, and any other available whole dried herbs by bundling them together and wrapping them tightly in cotton twine. Premade smudge sticks, usually crafted of white sage, are available at magic or herb shops and natural markets. You can also use a simple incense stick; sandalwood and nag champa are good choices. Before lighting your stick or bundle, ground and center. Ask the energies of fire, smoke, and herbs to cleanse your home and align you with your passion and purpose. Now walk through your house, wafting smoke over doors and windows, gathering places, and sacred spots like altars and the stove. Thank the spirits for cleansing your home.

# July 3

When the sun burns fierce and fiery, focus your energy on passion. In what ways do you express passion in your life? Take some time for creative expression. Paint, cook, garden, write, dance, sing—whatever calls to you. If your passion has been lacking of late, consider the following chant:

*I reclaim my fire, my passion.*
*The pleasure and the pain*
*that make me whole,*
*the light and the dark that burn within,*
*the power of creation*
*and destruction that are*
*granted me by the Goddess;*
*I reclaim these powers*
*I reclaim these powers*
*I reclaim these powers.[72]*

# July 4

In the United States, July 4 is a day of fire. Flames can burn, and they can transmute. Fire can be about passion, creativity, erotic energy, motivation, life energy, leadership, and mastery; fire is also about anger, overwhelming greed, and destruction. The difference lies in being able to direct fire energy. Wildland firefighters focus on fire "containment" rather than putting out every last flame. Fire dancers know the necessity of balance: fire-dancing tools and the dancer's body must be in perfect balance to be safe.

Journal about the energy of fire in your life. At this yang time of year, are you channeling the intensity of the sun, or are you burned out? Are you on fire with certain projects? How can you best contain and focus these energies to better serve yourself and the planet?

# July 5

Go outside and sit. Take some time to feel the earth.
Reach your attention down into the soil and out into
the air. What does the sun feel like? What energies can
you sense in the land? What animals, insects, and plants
surround you? "Psychic" or extended-sense communication with the land begins by listening deeply. It requires
quieting the mind. Taking time to sit helps attune you to
the energies of the land. This time of year, when the sun
is hot and fiery and the land awake and powerful, you
may find it easier to hear what it is saying. Write down
whatever sensations and words arose for you. What
have you learned by spending time with the earth?

One way to commune with the earth that has been used for thousands of years is to enter a trance state through the use of rhythm. Dancing, drumming, chanting, swaying, and even walking rhythmically attune the body's rhythms to natural earth rhythms. Brain waves shift, allowing us to tap into the dreamtime while awake. Go outside—you may have to wait till the cool of night—and drum or dance in whatever way works for your body. Let the earth's heartbeat dance with your own. Feel your body sink into a deeper sense of life and the Goddess. Listen. When you are finished, ground and center. Drink some tea or eat something to help you return to everyday life.

# July 7

Let's play! Go to a natural area—the backyard, the beach, a wilderness area, a park—and begin by walking or sitting to get into the rhythm of the land. When you are ready, allow yourself to play as you did when you were a child. Build forts or nests, climb trees, collect treasures, watch bugs up close. Allow yourself to slip into how it felt to be a child playing in nature.

Give yourself several hours or a whole day. Collect a few treasures to bring back with you: objects that will not harm the environment in any way, or maybe a memory, dance, or sound. Share that treasure and any other discoveries with someone else.[73]

# July 8

The Celtic month of Tinne, holly, begins today. It is a tree of the waning half of the year, for we have passed the summer solstice, and daylight hours are shortening. In Celtic mythology, the Oak King, who rules over the first half of the year, is killed by the Holly King, who rules from summer solstice until Yule, when the roles are reversed. Holly is another masculine tree for a masculine time of year, though botanically there are male and female holly trees. The female plant produces the berries, and you need one of each for fertilization.

The leaves boast sharp points, and the berries are poisonous. Holly is beautiful but must be approached with caution, a reminder that nature is wild and potentially dangerous.

What part of you is dying this time of year? What is replacing that old self? Journal about this change, calling on holly to guide you.

# July 9

You are always connected to the earth simply by breathing, pumping blood, drinking a tall glass of water, and eating food. On days when it is too hot (or rainy or snowy or whatever) to go outside for very long, reconnect with the earth by taking a moment to focus on your heart center. The heart is the strongest generator of electrical and magnetic energy fields in the body. Attuning to your heart center aligns you with the great pulse of the earth and all energy that surrounds you.

*Earth my body*
*Water my blood*
*Air my breath and*
*Fire my spirit!*[74]

# July 10

In November I wrote about the Via Negativa, the path to Spirit through darkness, suffering, and the void. In April you explored the Via Positiva, the path to God through light, dance, and joy. In May we played with the Via Creativa, the way of co-creation and giving birth. The final path to Goddess is the Via Transformativa, the way of transformation. We are transformed, and that leads us to transform the world. We do so through compassion and the pursuit of justice. The Via Transformativa is also a celebration of the other three paths' culmination. We are brought to our knees in celebration of the beautiful earth—of Soil, Soul, and Society—and we are called to give back. We are called to join "the dance of all creation in the quest for balance."[75]

What is transforming you—what has broken your heart, cracked it wide open, and called to you for change? How can you help transform it? Write about

transformation, and then name three things, big or small, that you could participate in to create greater balance in the world.

When we feel overwhelmed by the injustice of the world, we can respond in three ways: we can shut down, we can get mad and take action, or we can sit in stillness and let the river flow over and around us, letting it gently heal the pain and quietly guide us toward compassionate action.

Today, find a place to sit outside by water or a tree or an overlook—anywhere you can sit and have a quiet relationship with nature is fine. Just sit and give the pain you carry in your heart to the Goddess and the land.

# July 12

When you sat yesterday in quiet relationship with the Goddess, something caught your attention—a leaf, an animal, the way the wind blew—something big or small. Close your eyes and see or feel this thing again. Enter it with your awareness. Now draw what you experienced. You could draw the actual object, like the deer you saw munching grass, or just swathes of color and shape that come out of your hand as you sit in connection with the memory of a moment.

# July 13

The land knows nothing of money or politics. It can be affected by it, but it does not participate in these human constructs. Go outside or sit by a window where you can see a favorite tree or body of water. Sit with this being as your companion. Let the human ideas of money, politics, and fashion fall away. Find the part of you that is eternal. Sitting in companionship with this natural being can help you enter this space. When your mind drifts, bring yourself back to this eternal space. Sit for at least twenty minutes attuning with soil and soul.

# July 14

Sit with your journal and hold in your awareness two things: those issues that have called you to compassionate action by breaking your heart, and that eternal sense of your inner self you encountered yesterday. Now, holding these two energy centers in your awareness, write. Let it all flow out: questions, anger, sadness, eternity, calm, anything. See what emerges.

# July 15

The sun has great power this time of year. Those of us who feel that our beautiful earth and a livable future for her plants and animals—including humans—are more important than monetary wealth can call on the power of the warrior sun to change the way we currently conduct business on earth. Invest in community, gardening, and simple living. If you have financial investments, move your money to green energies like wind and geothermal. Remove your funds from fossil-fuel investments. Convert to solar. Ride your bike or save up to get a hybrid vehicle. We can do this.

# July 16

Go outside early in the morning and engage your senses. Smell the soil—get your face down close to the dirt and really smell it. Taste a berry, some dew, or a ripe tomato. Close your eyes and run your hands over different textures: a tree trunk, a stone, a feather. While your eyes are shut, listen. Give your entire body over to listening to wind, birds, insects, rain. Look at something that draws your attention, and then look closer. Look again. Engaging all your senses—smell, taste, touch, hearing, and sight—will help you fall in love with the land anew. When we live in love, we remember what we are here for.

## July 17

Here's another one from the pages of childhood:

Gather a collection of favorite flowers, and press them between sheets of paper in a large book or a flower press. You can make a simple flower press by piling together several sheets of paper and cardboard till your bundle is at least an inch thick, then secure with strips of Velcro, large clips, or rubber bands. Let the flowers and leaves dry for several weeks. When you take them out of the press, glue them to thick paper for cards and collages or preserve between sheets of contact paper to make a book mark or hang in a window.

# July 18

The Via Transformativa is about seeking balance in the world, but it requires maintaining balance in yourself. Over the past few weeks you have considered the world's injustices and overwhelming issues, balanced by falling in love with nature by cultivating delight. We need to do both. Our relationship with nature fuels and renews us. Our love of the earth inspires us to take action.

Make a list today of those areas in your life that need better balance. Know that you can serve the earth better when you are in balance—so today, list the ways you will balance your time, money, and other energies.

# July 19

Just as a garden needs healthy soil to grow, we humans need balanced, healthy energy to grow sturdy roots and robust fruit. We tend to frame the ways we could improve our health in negative ways: *I need to lose weight, cut out caffeine,* or *stop biting my nails.* These negatives are not very motivating, however. To identify positive actions toward better health, ask a big healthy tree for advice. Or if you live in a climate with few trees, find another natural being that exemplifies health, like a river or a mountain—or even a weed! They tend to be the healthiest of all. Sit by this healthy being, and attune with it by extending your awareness into its energy. Ask it aloud or in your mind what it has to say about health. Let it speak to you in sensations, images, or phrases.

# July 20

Caroline Myss writes that "healing is ultimately a mystical experience and not one that can be attained through the maneuverings of the mind."[76] Whether we are talking about healing the environmental crisis or our own bodies, we have to turn to Goddess for this mystical experience to occur. We have to let go of attachment to any outcome and open ourselves to the infinite power of the grace of God. What happens in your body when you read this? Does your sense of reason fight back, or do you settle into the non-rational yes? Write or meditate on the idea of healing as a mystical experience.

# July 21

A prayer for today:

Spirit, let me take what has happened in the world and transcend it. Let this crisis I am holding in my awareness transform me past the point where evil, despair, or destruction can destroy me. Help me to be stronger by responding to the world with a power greater than despair: the power of love.[77]

# July 22

Peat moss is often used to improve the tilth and water-holding capability of soil, but peat moss is not ecologically sustainable. It is gathered from bogs that took thousands of years to develop, and it is collected by draining the bog to let the peat dry out. Peat bogs are important ecosystems, containing animals and plants found only in peat bogs. They trap methane and carbon. They are not instantly renewable. Instead of peat moss, or the "eco" alternative coir (coconut hulls imported from tropical regions), use compost, leaf litter, composted manure, or dairy fiber, which is processed manure (http://www.highwayfuel.com/pp_dairy_fiber .html). To fluff clay, use gypsum instead of peat, which really doesn't do all that much fluffing anyway and has no nutrient value.

# July 23

The sun enters the astrological sign of Leo today. Leo the lion is ruled by the sun and tends toward expressiveness, power, and sometimes stubbornness. Beneath the fiery exterior, however, lies a hidden sensitivity as well as emotional idealism. Gold, rubies, and golden flowers are associated with this sign.

Today is a great day to make something. If you need a little more fire in your life at this time, call on Leo by crafting a painting in gold and ruby hues. Or if fire is a bit too prominent for you right now, get a massage focusing on the back and spine, where Leo can store pent-up energy.

# July 24

Do something for yourself today. We healers and dreamers can forget to care for ourselves, putting all our energies into caring for others and the earth. Get that massage you didn't get yesterday or go for a walk in nature by yourself or take an afternoon nap. Turn off the phone. Enjoy a cup of wine or tea with a friend. Drink iced lemon balm tea, which soothes and tones the nervous system. Buy a perfect piece of fruit and enjoy it drizzled with honey.

# July 25

In the modern Mayan calendar designed by José Argüelles, there are thirteen moon-based months; 28 days (a moon cycle) times 13 months equals 364 days, so July 25 (on the Gregorian calendar) is designated the Day Out of Time, "a day for sacred pause and cel-ebration before the dawning of the new year."[78] Today, meditate on sending love and gratitude to the planet. Feel yourself enter timelessness. Feel yourself connected to thousands of people in the international Thirteen Moon Calendar community who are committed to rais-ing the energy of the planet toward greater good.

# July 26

With the right balance of water, nutrients, and sun, a flowering plant will form a fruit, the tender, sweet parcel that first protects and then gives away its seed. Find out what fruits are in season locally by visiting a farmers' market or doing a search online for "fruit in season [your city or state]."

Choose a juicy, ripe fruit. Sit down with your fruit and smell it. An organic, locally grown fruit will smell just the way it should. Feel it with your fingers and your lips. Now close your eyes and take a bite. Chew slowly. Can you feel the sunlight on your tongue? Taste the soil and rain? Swish the juices around, tasting slowly in different parts of your mouth. What words come to mind? What images? Get to know this fruit like a new lover. Let it send tingles all the way down to your toes and open your heart to the gifts of the Goddess.

# July 27

The Latin roots for *fruit* include the meanings "delight" and "satisfaction." We tend to consider how fruits give *us* delight or how *we* are satisfied with the fruits of our labor. I wonder, though, how much the fruit gives the plant a sense of satisfaction. The Latin root for *satisfy* means to "discharge fully" and "enough." The plant has satisfied its charge. It has completed its purpose.

In what ways is your own purpose being satisfied or coming to fruition? To help you see your purpose and its fruit better, try making a bubble chart. Write your name in the middle of a page and circle it. Now draw lines out from this word to connect more words in bubbles that describe or identify you. Let those birth more words. When one or more of these words ignites an emotional response in you, start a new bubble chart with that word as the center. See what emerges.

# July 28

Your soulwork is the thing you would do even if you were not paid for it. It's the thing you think of when you awake in the morning. It's a kernel of energy, an image, a seed that fuels all you do. Your hobbies and paying job are then "delivery systems"[79] for this soul calling; they are not the calling itself, they just deliver that energy into the world as fruit flesh delivers a plant's seed.

Picture yourself as a piece of fruit. Imagine in your core a seed or pit glowing with life force. All around that core is the juicy, sweet flesh that is your work. Picture in your mind the words that arose in yesterday's exercise. How do the fruit and the words relate? Let them help you root in the center of your soulwork.

After you've begun to hear the call of your soul, it is time to leave the safety of the home. Some of us do this when we go away to college, but many do not. We cling to the teachings and identity of our childhood self even as we go out into the world as a "working adult." Until we shed that old self, however, we cannot truly be free to inhabit our true selves. A culture stuck in late childhood or adolescence is pathological, mired in "a way of life that emphasizes social acceptability, materialism, self-centered individualism, and superficial rather than authentic, intimate relationships."[80]

Notice today the images and messages you come across that value materialism and individualism over authenticity and intimacy. What do these messages do to you? What do they do to the earth?

# July 30

Leaving home and leaving the adolescent self (no matter one's chronological age) is frightening. It can take years, especially if we've no one to guide us. Turn to the earth as your elder. Let fruit on its journey to new tree-hood, the salmon on its journey to the ocean, and the monarch on its great migration be your guides.

Dance your journey. Start out as a seed and grow toward the sun. Move across the room toward adulthood. Be a salmon pushing toward the ocean. Become a butterfly high above the earth. Become a flower, a fledgling, a river. Dance out your story, and let it show you who you really are.

## July 31

Though the official start of fall and its autumn weather are still weeks off, we are slipping toward the end of summer. We are poised between the blazing heat of the sun and the bittersweet kiss of letting go. We've been focusing on the sweetness of fruit; today, let us honor the bitter.

If you still have any cool-season vegetables in your garden, they have probably gone to seed. When they do, in order to protect the seed until it is ready to carry on the plant's DNA, leafy parts turn bitter. While we tend to avoid bitter foods, including a little bitter in the diet aids digestion and the liver. Gather some bolted greens or another bitter green such as dandelion or mustard. Sauté in butter, garlic, and a little wine. Serve with something rich like meat or oily beans.

# Lammas

The first of three harvest festivals, Lammas honors the abundance of late summer. This abundance is evident in living plants and animals as well as the first deaths. We cut sheaths of wheat, pluck fruits from the vine, and dig up roots, killing other forms of life so that we may live. The end of summer approaches. For these reasons, Lammas is bittersweet.

*Lammas* in Anglo-Saxon means "loaf mass," a ritual to honor bread crafted of freshly cut grains. Another name for this holiday is the Gaelic Lughnasadh, which comes from the sun god Lugh. In many climates this is a time of heat and sun. It is a time to honor the ongoing harvest while we tilt ever so slightly toward the darker half of the year.

# August 1

Old English *hærvest* means "autumn," the period between August and November. Today we begin the harvest time, a busy and crucial period for our farming ancestors. The word *harvest* also has root meanings related to cutting, dividing, and gathering. In modern times we associate the beginning of August with ripening fruit, browning grass, and the slowing down of the height of summer as we prepare to return to school. The typical school year has its own roots in agricultural society as well: once the hardest work was complete and the silos and cellars full, the children could return to their own tasks of learning. Today children and adults alike sense this back-to-school energy, a return to the realm of mind now that the earth and the needs of the body have been tended to.

Sit beneath a tree or another natural spot that calls to you, and meditate on the energy in the earth and in your body as we collectively pull away from the visceral

summer and into the more cerebral autumn. How is this reflected in your daily life?

# August 2

Lughnasadh traditionally was celebrated when grains and berries were ready for harvest, which could fall anywhere from mid-July to mid-August, depending on the previous spring and summer's weather. The harvest, beginning now and ending sometime near Samhain, determined how a family or community would weather the coming winter. Today we no longer carry such a strong sense of the Wheel of the Year, where one season determines the next. We are less affected by the vagaries of weather than we once were, and this protection from the elements removes us from the natural flow.

Though we may not feel the impact of the Wheel in terms of food sources, we are still affected by the energies of the earth as it spins round the sun. Take some time to reflect on the past few seasons. Write in your journal about events that occurred last spring and summer. How are they affecting you now? What are you harvesting? How will this determine the next six months?

# August 3

What does abundance mean to you? Today, identify a
symbol of abundance, such as fruit, cash, or friendship.
Find a way to give that to others: donate at the local
food bank, give a cash donation to a favorite charity, or
have tea with a new friend who might be lonely. How
does it feel to give abundance to others? What other
ideas does this practice spark?

# August 4

All energy comes from the sun (or the supernova that created the sun, as in fusion). Coal, gas, and petroleum are energy from plants long dead, compressed, and cooked by the earth. When we burn massive amounts of these fuels, we create greater byproducts than the earth can process, aka pollution. Getting closer to the original energy source creates less byproducts; this is another way of saying that photovoltaic energy, wind power (wind comes from the heat of the sun moving air around), and plain old warmth from the sun are clean energies.

Ways to bypass fossil fuels and get close to using the sun directly include:

- · hanging your clothes out on a line to dry
- · drying tomatoes in the sun on a clean window screen

· cooking pizza on a solar oven made of
cardboard and aluminum foil (see http://www
.outdoorcook.com/article1046.php or search
"solar oven")

· eating veggies straight out of the garden,
transforming sun energy via plants to your
own life force

# August 5

The Celtic month of Coll, or hazel, begins today, bringing us the energy of wisdom. Coll's number is nine, which is the completion of a cycle, a time of wisdom. Hazel is traditionally associated with the salmon, who travels long and far, then returns with wisdom and strength to her birthplace, where she spawns the next generation. You are the salmon on her journey, seeking the wisdom of the hazelnut. Take a walk, sit in your yard, or enter the wilderness, and ask the land to share with you a lesson or symbol of wisdom. Journal about your discoveries, and pay special attention to your dreams.

# August 6

Depending on your first average frost date, now is the time to begin planting fall crops. The idea of fall planting is to get a cool-season plant nice and mature before the frost hits, when they will go dormant but not die. You can then harvest them for several more months; with the right setup, you can harvest all the way through even a cold and snowy winter. The trick is to plant seeds in a cool spot, since most cool-season seeds prefer cooler temperatures to germinate. Cover them with a row cover to shade them a little. When it starts to get cool, build them a cold frame or cover with plastic sheeting.

See September 10 for information on cold frames, and check out *Four-Season Harvest* by Eliot Coleman for more on fall planting.

# August 7

Chinese medicine considers late summer to be "the interchange of all seasons." Writes Paul Pitchford in *Healing with Whole Foods*, "It is the point of transition from yang to yin, between the expansive growth phases of spring and summer and the inward, cooler, more mysterious fall and winter seasons."[81] It is recommended that you choose harmonizing foods for each meal, which include mildly sweet, yellow or golden, and round foods. Food should have a mild flavor and be prepared simply. A mild fast of eating one grain only can help purify and cleanse.

A simple stir-fry can help align you with this transitional time. Try millet or rice topped with carrots, cabbage, peas, and garbanzo beans or tofu, followed up with a desert of cantaloupe.

# August 8

Find a source of water, anything from a dish filled with tap water to the ocean. Sit where you can see the sun reflecting off the surface of the water. If you are using a dish of water, give it a gentle push to get the water moving a little. If the light is too intense, move a little to one side so you get a reflection without hurting your eyes. The best place to do this is next to a pond or other large body of water, where the light is refracted into a million sparkles. Sit and watch the light, letting it move you into a trance state. You are light. The world is light. Feel yourself dissolving into the light.

When you are ready, look away from the light. Be sure to ground before returning to everyday life.

# August 9

One of the most commonly grown garden vegetables is the tomato. When grown by the home gardener, this tangy fruit bears little resemblance to the anemic supermarket variety and can come in many colors—from green to yellow to purple as well as the quintessential red. If you haven't any ripening in your garden this year, get some from a friend or farmers' market. Vine-ripened tomatoes are best; according to Paul Pitchford in *Healing with Whole Foods*, tomatoes picked green and ripened off the vine can weaken the kidney-adrenal function.

Tomatoes are cooling and alkalizing. They soothe the liver and aid digestion. They detoxify the body and purify the blood. They can relieve high blood pressure and headaches caused by liver heat.[82] Enjoy yours freshly sliced and sprinkled with fresh herbs like basil or oregano plus a pinch of sea salt. Or make pico de gallo by chopping up tomato with a bit of jalapeño, onion, and cilantro.

# August 10

Go to a farmers' market and buy yourself a feast. Farmers' markets often cost more than big grocery stores because the farmers grow smaller crops. They have to pay for fuel, water, and land, unsubsidized by government and fertilizer companies. By paying more to the farmer, however, you keep money local. You invest in the health of the land, the farmer, and your community's children. You get more wholesome food, and often you can find varieties of fruits and vegetables unavailable at the supermarket. You are therefore investing in your health, your connection with the land, and the future. You are also paying for better taste. Bring your cloth bags, ask about case discounts, and, to save money, shop at the end of the market or end of the season for the best deals.

# August 11

As we harvest the bounty of the land, we can also notice what we harvest in our spirit. What do you harvest at this time? Even though the Wheel keeps turning and there are many more seeds sprouting, vines twining, and flowers budding, in some areas of life we can harvest bounty. This is the first harvest, so the gifts of our work may be smaller than at other times, but just as zucchini is better small, so sometimes the little things are what matter. Write a list of all the things you harvest today: a success at work or with your children, a clean bathroom, a realization, or a new friend.

# August 12

The Perseid meteor shower, so named because it seems to radiate from the constellation Perseus, peaks on the night of August 12 into the wee hours of August 13. It has been viewed by humans since at least AD 36, when it was recorded by Chinese astrologers. Get away from city lights if you can, get in a comfortably reclined position, and stare at the stars. A star chart or smartphone app can help you locate Perseus, or you can just watch for stars.

I get vertigo contemplating the size of the universe into which I look, compared to the size of this planet and my life. I feel I am both a speck of nothingness and a radiantly crucial part of all that is.

# August 13

We're nearly halfway to September, which means the end of the high heat is in sight. If you're feeling drained, angry, or just too darn hot from all the yang, include a low-sugar sports drink or vitamin C–based electrolyte beverage in your day. Magnesium can help soothe sore muscles, and your regular multivitamin can be key in getting you through the draining month ahead. Herbal remedies for heat fatigue include lemon balm tea and burdock infusion or tincture, available at health-food stores. Of course, check with a natural-care practitioner if you have any concerns, but most of these remedies are safe for soothing the heat.

# August 14

*"Our sacred work is what nature-based traditions*
*call our giveaway to our people and place."*
· · · · · ·
Bill Plotkin[83]

We call it service, this giveaway. True service happens when you have a bounty you've harvested—your soul calling—and you give it to others in the service of the earth, either the land or the community (or both). This can happen only when the harvest is ripe. And then it just happens, if you let it—meaningful work brings you into meaningful relationship and service.

In what ways are you sharing your bounty? If you feel you have not yet identified a delivery system for your soul calling, spend some time brainstorming. You might write a blog, volunteer, take a part-time job, or incorporate elements of your soul calling into your current career.

# August 15

Do you have a bumper crop of something in your garden? Check out www.AmpleHarvest.org, which will help you donate your extra fresh produce to a local food pantry. Some organizations, like Denver's Yard Harvest (yardharvest.org) will even come harvest your fruit and donate it for you. You can also search "plant a row for the hungry + (your city)" to find a local organization.

"The opposite of hunger isn't full. It's healthy," says Gary Oppenheimer of Ample Harvest.[84] By sharing the bounty in service of others, we can help create healthy people and healthy communities.

## August 16

Today, a prayer:

Thank you, Goddess, for helping me see the fruits of my labors. My work has ripened on the vine, and now I am ready to pluck the sweet fruits and share them with others. I ask that you help me remember to rejoice in the harvest while holding my full basket up to you in gratitude and humility. So mote it be.

Everything in and on the earth was birthed as elements formed in the sun. Walk around your house, yard, or workplace, and touch things (or just look at them if you are in public and don't feel like involving others just now), saying aloud or in your mind, *from the sun*. Touch your heart center: *from the sun*.

# August 18

If you can stand turning on the oven, bake some corn-bread. If you cannot bear heating up the kitchen, try making it in a covered cast-iron pan on the grill. Corn nourishes the heart and kidneys and improves digestion. Fresh corn has more enzymes and vitamins than dried corn, so it is more like a vegetable than a grain and is "better suited to the warmer seasons and the robust person than the dried variety."[85] I like mixing fresh kernels into cornbread batter. Green chilies and a little cheddar or cotija are also tasty additions.

Most western Native American cultures have a corn goddess, such as Zaramama from Peru, Chicomecoatl of the Aztecs, and Selu of the Cherokee. Most of her names translate as Grain Mother or Corn Mother. Give thanks for her gift as you share a meal of maize.

# August 19

Climate change is here. On August 10, 2012, Reuters posted, "The worst U.S. drought in more than half a century has battered the corn and soybean crops with larger losses than expected, causing domestic stockpiles to shrivel to near bare-bones levels."[86] One way we can protect ourselves from global food shortages is to grow our own foods in our backyards and in our communities. The sustainable gardener and farmer needs to focus on open-pollinated, non-hybridized crops such as blue and red corn, quinoa, and heirloom vegetables. Variety and community are going to be keys to survival, so that no one heat-stressed crop is wiped out by opportunistic insects or bacteria, and no one people are left hungry.

Another way to protect yourself and family is to expand your diet beyond corn, wheat, and soybeans (which are in most processed foods). Enjoy some blue corn tortilla chips with quinoa salad for dinner. These

ancient foods have not been tampered with (as much) by agribusiness, and by purchasing and eating them you are supporting sustainable farming and biodiversity.

# August 20

Another thing that will help us as the climate destabilizes is the revitalization of traditional skills. Here's another place where community will be invaluable. Local farms and homesteading groups offer classes in skills like cheese making, wine making, bread baking, and raising your own food. Sewing, knitting, and carpentry are other skills useful in a community-centered economy.

Identify some new skills you want to learn. If you don't know where to begin, try searching online for "homesteading classes" and the name of your city. Botanic gardens and community gardens will often offer classes or lead you to them.

Then, to get yourself inspired to take some of those classes, try a simple and magical skill: making butter. Pour at least 2 cups raw or pasteurized (not ultrapasteurized) cream into a blender or food processor and

turn it on high. First you will make whipped cream, and then butter. The extra liquid can be used in baking (it's buttermilk, but the buttermilk used in pancakes and such has been fermented, so just add a little lemon juice to curdle it).

# August 21

*"O Lord, how manifold are thy works!*
*In wisdom hast thou made them all; the earth*
*is full of thy creatures...When thou sendest*
*forth thy breath, they are created."*
• • • • • •
Psalm 104

What *is* this divine breath? What is spirit, soul, life? This spark we share with oak trees, humpback whales, kitchen sage, and button mushrooms—what does it teach us about Goddess? If "nature is the embodiment of divinity,"[87] the creation of the Creator, it can cause us to know the Creator. Look today for signs of creativity in nature. It is literally everywhere.

# August 22

The word *inspiration* means "breathing in." The Hebrew word *ruah* and Greek *pneuma* mean both "breath" and "spirit." To get inspired, we must breathe in spirit. When seeking solutions to problems, turn to the wind and your breath for wisdom. Sit still and watch your breath, letting thoughts arise and blow away like leaves in the wind. Inspiration will drift gently into the stillness you create by simply breathing.

# August 23

Today is Vulcanalia, feast day of Vulcan, the Roman god of the sun, fire, volcanoes, and craftsmanship. This is a good day to transform something by fire. Find a local pottery shop that will allow you to make a clay vessel and fire it in their kiln. Or make a bonfire and toss into it an old piece of jewelry, maybe a ring from a previous marriage or earrings from a past phase of life. After the fire cools, pull out the charred metal and place it on your altar as a symbol of the power of fire to transform.

# August 24

The sun enters Virgo today. Virgo can either be meticulous or fussy, diligent or perfectionist. Usually Virgos vacillate between these poles. They can be prone to worrying and criticism, but they can also contribute to a group with their liveliness and practicality. These traits sound a lot like those working to bring balance to our environmental crisis. Take today to clean up your act. If there are any areas in your life where you have been meaning to "go green," do so today. Set up recycling, start a compost pile, get your bike fixed, change out old light bulbs—any of the "little" things that you just haven't gotten around to changing. Today is the day.

# August 25

People have been pickling vegetables for as long as we've had vinegar—the Babylonians used vinegar to preserve and pickle 7,000 years ago. Try your hand at making pickles or sauerkraut. If you've extra cucumbers, cauliflower, beans, or peppers in the garden, pickling is a fun way to preserve them. Or you can visit a farmers' market to buy small cucumbers, fresh dill, and garlic for the best dill pickles ever. For recipes, check your library for titles on preserving and pickling; *The Complete Book of Home Preserving*, edited by Judi Kingry and Lauren Devine, is one to try, or see Andrea Chesman's *The Pickled Pantry*.

# August 26

There is (of course) a smartphone app designed to help you find extra fruit to harvest for free, called Neighborhood Fruit. The designers also have a website and blog at neighborhoodfruit.com. The app costs 99¢ at the time of this writing, and the website is free to join and use.

From the website:

> Neighborhood Fruit is a service that helps people find and share the fruits, nuts, and vegetables growing within their communities. The site features interactive maps of backyard bounty and abundance growing on public land ...
>
> · share the fruit from your yard
> · add a tree on public land to the map
> · find abundance in your neighborhood
> · learn more about unusual fruit

· Explore on the go with Find Fruit, the iPhone app companion to the site!

Craigslist.org is another place to look; go under your city, then click "free" and search "fruit" or the specific kind of fruit you want. No one wants to see the fruit from their trees go to waste, and few people can eat or preserve all the fruit on a tree by themselves.

# August 27

The Old English name for August was *Weodmonað*, meaning "weed month." Weeds that have braved the heat of summer and avoided the gardener's tug tend to be robust and hard to eliminate. Watering first or weeding after a rain, then pulling in a sunwise direction (clockwise in the Northern Hemisphere) helps get rid of weeds. Put them all in their own compost tumbler. In the spring when they have composted, pour the compost into a burlap sack, put in a bucket, and make compost tea by covering the sack with water and letting it steep for a day (no longer—it gets horribly nasty). Throw away the compost and pour the tea on your garden. This way you reuse your weeds—which are high in nutrients needed in your climate—but don't spread the seeds, which will likely not be destroyed by composting.

# August 28

I notice a lot of spiders this time of year. They climb up the drains to get out of the heat, spread their webs across pathways, and nestle egg sacks in every nook and cranny. Spider teaches us about weaving the patterns of life and creativity. She connects us to our ancestors. She is a warrior, but she knows how to wait for what will come to her. Spider also teaches us about respect for nature. Spiders are nearly everywhere, but we don't always realize their presence. They may frighten us even as we respect them for being important parts of the ecosystem.

When you see a spider today, thank her for reminding you about balance and respect. You may be feeling a lack of creativity, and Spider is reminding you to get your own web spinning. Call on Spider's creativity, cunning, and clarity to awaken your own inner weaver.

# August 29

At Native American potlatches and powwows, wealth is shown not by how much you have but by how much you can give away. To honor a special event like a birthday, it is customary to give a donation to a cause (at a powwow it would be to the tribe) in honor of the occasion. For a bigger event like the birth of a child, you would host a giveaway. Items related to food or shelter—blankets, baskets of food, household supplies—are given to the community in a ritual fashion.

When you give extra jars of canned fruit to neighbors, apples to a food pantry, or blankets and coats to a homeless shelter, do so with honor in your heart. This is a sharing of the blessings you have in your life. Let it be a ritual giving. Give thanks for the opportunity to share your wealth.

# August 30

Scraps and weeds to be thrown into the compost need to be chopped up small to hasten transformation into soil. This is what we do when we dissect a life experience so that we can learn from it. Take something you are ready to let go of and transform—a life event, something someone said, a traumatic experience—and write words or draw images of chunks of the event. For example, maybe the birth of your child was more invasive that you had planned. Write down "nurse with red hair," "IV line," "helplessness." Or draw a picture of the line on the heart monitor, the flower in the vase by your bed, and the top of your baby's head. Take these images and words and bury them in your garden compost or the backyard or even a houseplant's pot. Ask that the Mother transform them into fertile soil.

# August 31

Transformation happens in surprising ways. We need not keep our compost in a pile in the corner of the garden, for instance. On May 21 you made a trench composter, digging a hole and burying scraps to amend the soil in place. You can also use compost materials as mulch, putting them right on your garden beds and covering them with something prettier like grass clippings. Or you can create a lasagna, or layered, compost bed, a great way to create a raised bed. You can plant fall crops in it right now, or let it cook over the winter and plant in a rich bed of soil in spring.

Lasagna gardening, by the way, doesn't mean planting tomatoes, basil, and spinach. It means creating a soil bed out of layered materials, as you would prepare a pan of lasagna. To create a layered compost bed, clear an area you want to turn into compost of weeds that have gone to seed. Put down cardboard or several layers of newspaper, and get this wet so it doesn't blow away. Add seedless weeds and kitchen scraps, followed by a layer of soil, then a layer of straw, then grass clippings, then soil, then manure, then dog hair, then more kitchen scraps and so on, until your pile is a foot or more deep. Water it, and let it sit.

Sometimes your inner transformation happens the same way, layers of life experience given a kiss of grace, when everything clicks and you have a fertile bed in which to plant seeds.

# September 1

The fall is a good time to plant trees and shrubs. Cooler temperatures and increased moisture make it a better time to plant than summer, and by planting them now you give their roots a chance to develop before spring. Also, many nurseries put their trees on sale this time of year. Visit a local nursery to ask what grows well in your area. If you haven't room in your yard, ask a local school if you can help kids plant trees on the school grounds.

# September 2

The Celtic month of Muin, often associated with grape-vines, begins today. *Muin* is more closely translated as "a thicket of thorny plants" and probably refers to black-berries.[88] Muin is about joy and exhilaration, and it is often connected to wine-laced revelry. But learning of its more direct translation brings up a different sort of joy for me. One of my great joys as a child in the Pacific Northwest was picking sun-warmed blackberries and eating them right off the vine. Just recently we planted two blackberry vines in our Colorado garden, bringing to my adult home a childhood joy. What will bring you joy today? If you cannot engage fully in that activity, such as picking buckets of wild blackberries, how can you create some small aspect of that joy?

## September 3

I always picture the word *September* as being brown, even though where I grew up it is a pretty green month. Autumn is written in varying shades of brown and orange. We like to dress in autumnal shades—olive, brown, burnt orange. Mostly we consider these colors coming from changing leaves. But it's not just leaves—notice how fall flowers come in shades of dark marigold, maroon, and orange. In dry lands, scrub brush turns dusty brown and sage. Ornamental kale is purple and dusty jade. Grass is the color of mustard. Fall fruits, too, are reds, plums, and deep greens. What fall colors do you see? Buy yourself a new box of crayons (they are on sale this time of year!) and play with the autumnal palette you see outside.

# September 4

Bring a camera to the farmers' market or on a hike. How many colors and shapes can you find? Look for textures and light. Notice how an eggplant is not just purple but also streaked with white. Find a pile of heirloom tomatoes, with their ugly bumps and diverse colors. Peaches and apples, too, are mottled and streaked. Can you see where one color turns into another?

If you are using a digital camera or phone, zoom in on your pictures. Set the blend of colors as your wallpaper on your phone, or print a few pictures and put them up on the refrigerator.

# September 5

How can you involve your community in greening projects? A project to connect neighbors could be as simple as exchanging garden produce. You could offer the corner of your yard for composting, collecting everyone's grass clippings and bug-chomped apples to transform into soil, which can then be redistributed or simply used in your garden to grow more food for your neighbors. Maybe there is an empty lot on your street that could be turned into a community garden and play space, or an existing park that could use some planter boxes of lettuces and tomatoes. Host a seed-sharing party, or offer to teach others about raising hens. The key to healing our people and the earth is through community action, big and small.

# September 6

On a gray day, go outside or park yourself in front of a big window and stare at the sky. Is the sky a wash of gray? What kind of gray? Are there eddies and bumps in the clouds, patches of blue sneaking through, areas that are darker, areas that are light? Notice that deep breath you take, the way your shoulders drop a little. We rarely let ourselves just stare at the clouds. When we do, though, nature reminds us who we are.

# September 7

In *Voices of the Earth* I wrote about the explosion on Whatcom Creek in Bellingham, Washington, which occurred on June 10, 1999, when gasoline leaked onto the creek and ignited. Three boys died, and all of the life in the creek for three miles was incinerated. Twenty-six acres of trees burned. A task force to restore the creek was formed with federal and state agencies and the local tribe. In 2009 a study was done of how the restoration had fared ten years later.

Ninety-five percent of the replanted trees that remained had doubled in height (some, due to normal competition for resources, had died). Aquatic insects rapidly returned, though the species were slightly different than before. "Deer, mink, and beaver are commonly observed along Whatcom Creek, as are tracks and scat of otter, coyote, raccoons, and other small- to mid-size mammals," reports a post-fire study. There are no major

areas of erosion due to the fire. Water quality and temperature do not seem to have been terribly affected.[90]

In short, the creek is rebuilding itself through help from humans. Our efforts do make a difference.

Is there a creek near your house that needs help? Contact your local city, parks department, or water board to find out how to volunteer to help with restoration efforts.

# September 8

When you plant seeds or save them from a plant to use
next spring or eat a plant, any plant, you are eating a
story. You are eating a chain of life, handed down, sometimes literally, by generations of people. In the age of
huge automated farms and fluorescent grocery stores,
we've mostly forgotten this. When you eat your dinner,

say a prayer of thanks for the story on your table. Share with your children the idea that plants came from seeds that came from plants back through millennia. Point out how people cultivated these plants over thousands of years until this one you eat tonight came to be.

# September 9

Some studies have found that microgreens, tiny greens just past the point of "sprouts," contain more nutrition than mature plants.[92] They are easy to grow indoors just about any time of year or in a cold frame in spring or fall. Fill a pot or planter (or even an old roasting pan) with potting soil. Sprinkle a mix of seeds, including mustard greens, radishes, lettuces, kale, beets, and basil, onto the soil, and pat down. Water lightly, and cover with plastic wrap (or a plastic grocery bag cut flat). When the greens sprout, remove the plastic and keep them moist. Cut the greens when they are an inch or two tall, and toss them into salads and stir-fries.

# September 10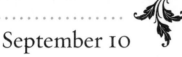

This is a good time of year to build a cold frame or hoop house, a way to extend your garden's growing season and get fresh vegetables year-round. Picture a tiny, unheated greenhouse that will raise the temperature of your garden bed just enough that your plants can make it through a cold winter. If you live in a warmer climate, you may not need such protection (and in fact, in places like Los Angeles, you are now beginning your garden instead of wrapping it up like the rest of us in North America), but in cold winter areas a cold frame is a little piece of miracle. We are using the sun and a little glass or plastic to harvest year-round.

An easy cold frame is a storm window covering a raised bed—be sure to prop it up for ventilation on warm days. Another simple and effective harvest extender is a hoop house or greenhouse made of a wooden or plastic frame covered in plastic sheeting. Put

it over kale, lettuce greens, and mache to extend their growing season. Search "cold frame" online or see the fabulous *Four-Season Harvest* by Eliot Coleman for more information.

# September 11

When disaster strikes, people unite to take care of one another. We focus on making sure our neighbors have enough food and a safe place to sleep. We are filled with fear that reality is no longer what we thought it was, and one way to deal with this fear is to care for others. We are jolted into aliveness, a state that yields compassionate action for others.

As the planet's climate changes, bringing many disasters and changes in what we thought equaled reality, we will see the positive power of humanity. Light a candle today for the interconnections among people, ingenuity, and compassion that arise in the face of crisis.

# September 12

When I was in college, I collected autumn leaves and taped them to my slanted bedroom ceiling in the shape of a spiral. There is something about fall that inspires childlike crafting and creating. Give in to that impulse today. Decoupage fall leaves to a box in which to store treasures discovered on your walks—treasures of the season like pine cones, stones, and dragonfly wings. To decoupage, paint both sides of a leaf with glue or Mod Podge, then press onto the box. When it dries completely, cover with another coat of glue. Or print a plain canvas bag with leaves; cover leaves with acrylic or fabric paint in shades of red, brown and orange, then press the leaf onto the canvas and carefully peel it off (practice on the inside of the bag first till you get the technique down).

# September 13

Another traditional fall activity that will get you feeling all autumn-y is making applesauce. Buy firm organic apples or harvest them from local trees. Peel them (optional), and cut them into chunks. Put them into a slow cooker, leaving only a couple of inches of space at the top, and pour in several cups of water (you can always add more if it gets dry). Sprinkle in some cinnamon and turn on the slow cooker. Let the sauce cook to a desired consistency, about five hours. If it's too soupy, remove the lid and put it on high to evaporate some of the liquid. Pour into clean glass jars and store in the fridge.

# September 14

As the nights cool, the crickets slow down their chirping. Instead of the frantic drive of summer calling, they trill long and slow and sleepy. Besides turning leaves, what do you observe that tells you we are slipping toward autumn? Some climates will already be quite cold; others get more rain, and dew covers the grass each morning. Your climate might be warm and balmy still, but the entire planet is changing seasons in subtle and not-so-subtle ways. What signs do you see, hear, smell, and sense?

# September 15

In preparation for Mabon, make a basket out of items in your yard or neighborhood that you can store fruits and nuts in or put on the altar. It need not be large or fancy, just handmade. To weave a basket, you need long, flexible material like grapevines, willow branches, suckers (the soft branches that grow around the base of trees and shrubs), or reeds (if you haven't anything you can use, you can buy grape and willow at craft stores). Strip the branches of leaves, tossing them into the compost. Soak in warm water if they are not soft enough (this makes a lovely smell if you are using willow). Cut four sticks at least a foot long and cross them to look like the Wheel of the Year—one horizontal, one vertical, and two crossing these. Weave a small, flexible vine around the base to secure them. Keep this weave as tight as possible, and tuck the end in to secure. Now gently bend up the supports to make a bowl shape, and begin weaving the material under and over the central support sticks, starting at the middle and working your way out. Keep it tight. When you come back to the stick you started on, the weaving material should go opposite the last pass, so weave on the inside if the last layer wove to the outside. Keep going, tucking in the ends, until you reach the top, tugging the supports up into your bowl shape as you go. Finish the basket by wrapping a small-in-diameter vine or grass in a spiral all around the top few vines.

For step-by-step photos, visit acornpies.blogspot .com/2009/04/how-to-make-little-willow-basket.html.

# September 16

Host or help organize a cooking party. Everyone brings their extra zucchinis, winter squash, apples, and other produce, plus any cases of food procured at the end-of-season farmers' markets or local farms opening their fields at harvest time. Over tea, come up with a few recipes (this might be a preliminary meeting before you cook or be figured out via email or Facebook). As a group, prepare a few meals for each family, plus a couple extra to bring to families with new babies or recent surgeries. If you are a part of a parenting group or a church, find out who needs extra help, any food allergies or special diet preferences they have, and whether they prefer visits or can put a cooler on the front porch for people to drop off meals.

# September 17

This is a great time of year to visit a nature center, many of which have trails and waterways, interpretive centers, and nature programs for all ages. Let yourself linger in the nature center, even if you don't have children. Peek into microscopes, pick up a map, and ask the interpreters what wildlife has been seen lately and the best trails to take this time of year. Sign up for a class or a nature hike, or check out books from their library.

To find a nature center near you, search online "[your city] nature interpretive center" or ask at the local library.

# September 18

In many habitats, wildlife is preparing for winter. Bears procure dens, squirrels hide nuts, and geese take wing for southerly lands. In what ways are you tucking in and slowing down? Get your den ready for winter by sweeping the front porch and removing summer cobwebs. Smudge the front door and ask for blessings upon the house as you enter the cooler months.

# September 19

If you planted sunflowers last spring, cover the flower heads with paper bags to protect them from birds. Leave a few uncovered to share. Squirrels will often chew the flowers over from the base; watering the ground around the flowers with urine or blood meal may deter them. Sunflower seeds are high in zinc, which is good for male health and generally fighting colds, and they are warming, making them a great snack on a cool fall day.

# September 20

A simple preserved fruit that makes a perfect Yule gift is rumtopf, a German compote. Layer cherries, stone fruits, and red currants in the bottom of a canning jar that has been sterilized in a boiling water bath. Sprinkle a thin layer of sugar on top of each layer of fruit. As you build your layers, focus your intention for this treat: *let it bring sweetness to the lives of those I give it to; let its sweet richness bring them true wealth; let them glow with the health of many fruits.* Pour dark rum over all the fruit layers. Cover the jar with a layer of plastic wrap or a clean plastic bag for an airtight seal, then add a tight lid. Let sit till Yule, then serve with ice cream, shortcake, pork, or pancakes. Strain off the liquid and add it to champagne, or drink it as a cordial. If little bubbles start to develop, it's fermenting; add 151-proof rum to halt fermentation.

# September 21

Make a devotional practice or ritual out of putting the land to bed. Spread the compost on garden beds and rake piles of leaves to make leaf mold (composted leaves—see September 29), contemplating what you need to tuck away for composting inside yourself. Collect any seeds from lettuce, orach, peppers, and squash, letting them dry before tucking them safely away for spring. What seeds do you tuck inside yourself to germinate after the cold stratification of winter? Mulch berry bushes and garden paths, which will protect the land from fall rain while retaining moisture and building the soil. Consider what needs protecting in yourself. Check your tools, oiling and repairing and carefully storing them. Let go, tuck in, protect. Consider how these practices reflect your inner self as well.

# *Mabon*

The autumn equinox is also called Mabon, after the Welsh god of love and youthful strength. He is a sun god, honored at this time as night and day sit momentarily in balance before slipping toward darkness. At Mabon, the Goddess evolves from mother to crone and the God prepares for death. The land is ripe, full of bounty; this is the Pagan Thanksgiving. It is a cooling, bittersweet holiday, for the bounty of ripe apples will fall, the leaves turn and drift to the ground. The sleep of winter is near.

We are leaving the energy of fire and entering the teachings of mystery and darkness. It's time to wrap up any loose ends from the heightened yang of summer and prepare for the gifts of autumn. Traditionally we put up food for winter, repair thicker blankets and quilts that have been stored since spring, and stack firewood high.

# September 22

Host a Thanksgiving feast this Mabon. If you eat meat, cook a local, free-range bird or beast, like a wild turkey, sustainably raised bison, or wild-caught salmon. If possible, purchase it directly from the fisherman, hunter, or farmer, or procure it yourself. Include local nuts, fruits, herbs, and vegetables in your meal. Light local beeswax candles in autumnal shades, and include a centerpiece of flowers and weeds from your area. Some mead, wine, or local beer adds a nice touch; this is the meal to splurge a little, bringing local opulence to the table.

# September 23

The sun enters the sign of Libra today. Fairness, justice, and diplomacy are important Libran traits. They are also key factors of our environmental movement and environmental justice. When the earth suffers, the planet's poor and nonhuman residents suffer the most.

For ways to protect the rights of all people regardless of income, race, or nation, visit Earth First! Newswire at http://earthfirstnews.wordpress.com/ or Cultural Survival and Global Response at http://www.cultural survival.org.

# September 24

Chinese medicine teaches us that autumn has an abundant and contracting nature. We turn inward and gather together. Leaves, fruit, and nuts fall from the trees as green recedes from the earth. Cook foods with less water and at lower heat for longer periods of time. Gradually incorporate more salty, sour, and bitter foods into your diet. Make a big pot of applesauce today; apples help cleanse the colon and lungs, which are organs associated with fall. Serve with a little horseradish (if you can stand it), gently cooked cabbage, and tempeh or pork. All of these foods will help you align with the energies of autumn.

# September 25

In the Northern Hemisphere, wine grapes are harvested between the months of August and October. Find a local winery through http://www.allamericanwineries. com/AAWMain/locate.htm or searching "(your city or state) + winery." Look for organic wines, which use only organically approved pesticides on the grapes or no chemicals at all. Taranga Creek winery in New Zealand wrote on their website, "In a recent investigation, the New Zealand Food Safety Authority (NZFSA) tested a variety of grapes found in supermarkets and found 26 different chemicals, with one grape sample containing 10 different residues."[93] These chemicals have been shown to be associated with cancer, endocrine disruption, and neurological disorders. The pesticides also disrupt the natural ecosystem in and around wineries. Organic wines contain fewer sulfides, a form of salt used in preservation, to which a growing number of people

are developing allergies. Also, many people feel organic wines taste better. In wine shops, look for the Certified Organic label. Local wineries may not be certified but may use fewer or no chemicals; call before you tour or buy to ask the owner how they grow their grapes. As you sip your local, organic varietals, say a toast to Dionysus or Bacchus, gods of wine, revelry, and regeneration.

## September 26

Basil, rosemary, cilantro, and chamomile don't do well when nighttime temperatures freeze, so harvest them now and preserve them. Herbs can be hung upside down to dry or be blanched and frozen in baggies or containers. Freezing tender herbs like basil and cilantro preserves more of their flavor and chlorophyll. Hardier herbs like sage and thyme do well dried. Herbs for teas, such as lemon balm, chamomile, and mint, can also be dried, then crumbled up and stored in airtight jars.

# September 27

As we enter the mysteries of autumn, our dreams begin to speak of the descent into the unconscious. Shadows lurk in the coolness of dusk and the shortening days. Our thoughts turn to Samhain, just over a month away, the time when we face death. When you begin to feel this pull toward the shadow and mysteries of the self, create a ritual that honors your need to go into this introspective place. Cast a circle or simply sit in a safe place where you will not be disturbed. Ground and center by feeling the earth and witnessing your breath.

As you breathe, notice if your breath gets caught somewhere—maybe your throat or your belly, or perhaps the top of your rib cage feels stuck. Picture this space beckoning to you, inviting you to follow it down a path and into a cave or a clearing of fall trees. Feel it pull you along on a spider's web. Follow. Keep breathing. Let it speak to you in images and sensations. What messages does it have for you? Keep coming back to that spot. Breathe.

When you are ready, walk back along the path, open your eyes, and come back to the present moment. Open your circle if you cast one. Drink a cup of tea or jump up and down. Write about your meditation in your journal.

# September 28

Make a simple immune-supporting tea by mixing 1 part elderberries, 2 parts echinacea, 1 part red clover, and ½ part usnea (oak moss). A "part" can be any measurement—a pinch, a handful, a measuring cup. Store in an airtight jar and make a tea by covering 2 tablespoons with 8 ounces boiling water (or make it to the strength you desire). Sweeten with honey, stevia, or licorice root if desired. You can find most of these herbs at health food stores that carry bulk herbs or from an herbalist; you can also order them online. LivingEarthHerbs.com and MountainRoseHerbs.com offer organic, locally sourced herbs. Or search "[your city] organic bulk herbs."

# September 29

Create a leaf litter compost pile. Leaves decompose with the aid of fungi in a slightly different process from the microbes that create compost. Small amounts of leaves in compost add nitrogen and organic matter, but for large amounts of deciduous leaves, it's better to create a pile separate from the compost. Otherwise the leaves stick together and decompose at different rates from the rest of the compost, leaving you with clumps of soggy leaves. Pick an out-of-way-corner of your yard to pile up fall's leaves. Wet them and leave them alone. In a dry climate you may want to cover the pile with a tarp or store them in a compost bin (without other organic matter). Let the pile rot for a year or more. The resultant fertilizer is called leaf mold. It contains, pound for pound, twice the mineral content as manure. Spread it on the garden in the spring; brassicas like cabbage and broccoli especially like composted leaf mold.

# September 30

Today begins the Celtic month of Gort, ivy, which is about resurrection and the labyrinth of the self as we spiral along our journey. Phoenix McFarland writes that "the Greeks presented a wreath of ivy to newly-weds as a symbol of fidelity."[94] To what do you pledge fidelity, otherwise known as devotion? How has this book helped you clarify your work as a soul living on our precious Earth? In meditation, see yourself walking through a doorway shrouded in ivy. On the other side is a temple dedicated to your life's work. What do you discover through the veil of ivy?

# October 1

The price of hay has gone up dramatically because of drought induced by climate change. It's becoming too expensive to feed cattle, horses, and other livestock that rely on hay. Help a local farmer by buying a bale or two of hay to feed his or her animals. Nonprofit agencies that rescue abandoned and abused horses and other farm animals also need help. If you don't know who to help, ask at a local feed store or call the local university extension office.

# October 2

> *Creativity belongs to the artist in each of us. To create means to relate. The root meaning of the word art is 'to fit together' and we all do this every day.*
> • • • • • •
> Corita Kent[95]

A not-too-scary way to make "real" art is with acrylic paints. Craft stores carry affordable tubes individually and in sets. Canvas comes in many sizes and prices, too. Treat yourself to a canvas or two and some acrylic paints. You'll also need some paint brushes made for acrylics.

Paint whatever comes to mind—fall colors, memories of October in childhood, a plant on the back porch, or just swirls of color. If any images or words linger from your body-focused meditation on September 27, paint them. Don't worry about how it looks. Let this be an exercise in how it feels to play with the creamy, colorful paints.

# October 3

All of life is the transformation of carbon molecules from extinct cycads and dinosaurs to molecules stored in soil, spread around the planet in water and air, and ingested by billions of organisms across time and land. Animals eat plants, plants eat animals, animals eat animals, plants eat plants. Death is not only about ending, it is about relationship. It is a graduation from one form to the next.

Notice today what has died, what has graduated—warm days, leaves, your dinner, a passage of life. Honor the relationships these deaths illustrate. Write, draw, or paint what you observe, or discuss your thoughts with a loved one over a glass of red wine.

# October 4

If weather allows it, do some yoga outside. Stretch high toward the trees, stand centered and grounded in mountain pose, and sink deep into down dog as the energy of the earth pulls you toward its center. Feel your energetic roots reach deep for nourishment. Many urban parks offer yoga and tai chi classes outside; contact your local parks and rec for listings or suggestions. Simply performing gentle stretches outside with bare feet will align you with the energies of the season.

# October 5

The corvids—ravens, crows, magpies, and jays—often come up in autumn and Samhain imagery, for they represent the transition from life into death. They are omnivores and enjoy a good scavenge of roadkill. They are intelligent birds with complex social structures and even language. Jamie Sams and David Carson in *Medicine Cards* regard raven as a bringer of magic and change in consciousness. Crow teaches us about sacred law and mystery.[96] *The Druid Animal Oracle* attributes to ravens the medicine of healing, initiation, and protection. "[Initiation] marks the death of one thing, which gives way to the birth of another." Raven helps you resolve opposites, "the very deepest form of healing."[97] When you see these birds or images of them, acknowledge what is being initiated and transformed in you. Send compassion to any fear you feel as you heal and evolve.

## October 6

Notice the angle and quality of the light halfway between Mabon and Samhain. When does the sun first peek through your windows in the morning? What is the angle of light at midday? When the sun reflects off any remaining leaves on trees and shrubs, at what angle does it hit? Notice and record your observations.

# October 7

Besides pumpkins, you can carve turnips (not hollowed out), other squash (how about those gigantic zucchini?), apples, and potatoes. Use sharp knives, tools for linoleum-block carving, or even small power tools to carve faces and images into your vegetables. Put them on the front stoop like your jack-o'-lantern, carve them into candle holders for the Samhain table or altar, or use them as a centerpiece for the Halloween party refreshment table. Give your carvings to the compost, chickens, or squirrels after Samhain.

# October 8

Pumpkins are great for more than carving. While small pumpkins are best for baking, any pumpkin can be eaten. Cut into halves or quarters, scoop out the insides, and bake skin-side up at 350 degrees for about 45–60 minutes (depending on how big it is) or until really soft. When the flesh cools, scoop it out and keep in the refrigerator or freezer until ready to use. For a smoother texture, blend the cooked flesh before using in recipes. Pumpkins relieve edema and eczema, help balance blood-sugar levels, and benefit the pancreas. Make into soup, muffins, and breads in addition to pie.

Save the seeds for munching, or let them dry and thread onto cotton string. Hang the seed garland outside for birds and squirrels, or grind up dry seeds and include in Samhain incense.

October is a time to put down roots. Store root vegetables like beets, carrots, and kohlrabi in the ground or in a root cellar. Eat root vegetable stews to take in the nourishment of the plant's root, which helps ground you. Also feel the ground beneath you, the land on which you live, and feel your roots reaching into the soil. Now is not a time to move or to strike out; rather, it is a time to gather in energy. If you're feeling restless, bring into your home fall-colored candles and accents like pillows or curtains the color of roots: golden, dark red, brown. Honor feelings of rootedness; if you don't feel like going out or staying up late, don't. Listen to your body responding to the energies of the sun and the earth at this deepening time.

# October 10

Wrap young trees and those with thin bark with tree wrap or another light-colored material to prevent sun scald over the winter, when leaves do not provide enough shade to protect them from the sun. Put rodent barriers around the base of young trees to protect them from hungry mice, voles, and rats. Young evergreens also need protection from dry and cold winter winds; a burlap screen on the windward sides will protect them. Mulch perennials with wood chips and straw to protect their roots from heaving and frost.

As you tuck in the garden for winter, wrap your plants as you would your children. Soak in the nourishing calm of wrapping and protecting the land.

# October 11

Another animal messenger who shows up this time of year is Spider. In August we saw Spider as a creator, reminding us to weave our own creative webs. This time of year, though, Spider is about our entry into the mystery. The spider's eight legs evoke the never-ending flow of infinity, a figure eight turned on its side.

Some spiders can mean death. If you've ever encountered a poisonous spider, you will understand how the closeness of death jolts us to be more alive. Even harmless spiders are startling, dashing out before us—*wake up!*

Spider teaches us about transforming fear. A friend of mine got a black widow tattoo on her wrist because they terrify her. The tattoo reminds her to awaken her warrior self.

How is Spider showing up for you these days? What message does she have for you?

# October 12

The power of apple, according to Scott Cunningham, is love and healing. Cinnamon brings us protection, healing, and passion, while clove drives away hostile and negative forces. Warm yourself a cup of apple cider—real cider, not the stuff in a sugar-infused packet. Add a cinnamon stick and a few whole cloves. Hold the steaming mug in your hand and meditate on health, protection, and positive energies. As you sip your drink, consider how passion is expressed in your life at this time.

# October 13

The last of the warm-season plants will be dying back about now. Chop them up and leave in place as mulch, covering with straw if you like. Or chop them up and put them in the compost. Tomatoes can be ripened in paper bags or by hanging the entire plant upside down in a cool but not frozen place. Or make a southwestern stew with green tomatoes, the last of the cilantro, tomatillos, green chilies, corn or hominy, and chicken or seitan.

As you continue to put the garden to bed for winter, feel a sense of the Goddess retreating into the Underworld. Let yourself turn inward as well.

# October 14

Animals prepare for winter by changing color, growing a thick coat, hibernating, or migrating. Is there a part of you that longs to take off this time of year, or do you long to crawl into a den and sleep for months? Perhaps you feel an urge to stock up, filling the pantry with root vegetables, nuts, and grains. Many of us delight in changing our summer coats to deeper colors and warmer coats, even in more temperate climates. Children go to bed more easily as the daylight hours shorten, and they may be harder to rouse in the mornings. We adults, too, tend to drink just one more cup of coffee or tea to get us going in the dim early light. How can you honor these natural urges to hibernate, migrate, or shift to meet the coming months? Are there changes to your schedule that could accommodate these feelings, or do expectations of yourself need to relax a little?

# October 15

Last November, as the Goddess searched the Underworld and prepared for the return of the light, we explored death and letting go. Now, again, we near Samhain. In what ways are the themes of letting go and release coming up for you? You may want to revisit meditations of death from nearly a year ago (October 31 and November 2 and 6) or reread your journal entries from these dates. How have you changed since then? What have you let go of, and what still binds you? Smudge yourself with white sage or another preferred herb, and offer prayers on the smoke for release and movement toward deeper integrity.

## October 16

Today is World Food Day. Visit http://www.worldfood dayusa.org/ to learn about this day, designed to increase awareness, understanding, and action to alleviate world hunger.

One way to participate in World Food Day is to join the powerful mission of Heifer International by giving livestock, bees, and other sustainable animal gifts to those in need. For as little as $20 you can help end world hunger and promote sustainable living.

From Heifer's website:

> With gifts of livestock and training, Heifer projects help families improve their nutrition and generate income in sustainable ways. We refer to the animals as "living loans" because in exchange for their livestock and training, families agree to give one of its animal's offspring to another family in need. It's called

Passing On the Gift—a cornerstone of our mission that creates an ever-expanding network of hope and peace.

They also have a fabulous education program for preschool through middle school. Learn more at www .Heifer.org and find a way to get involved.

# October 17

An easy and versatile nondairy creamy soup can be made with potato, onion, broth, a little cashew butter (use SunButter if you're allergic to nuts), and any other vegetables of your choosing. Sauté a diced onion and a little salt in a little butter, chicken fat, or oil till translucent. Add 1–2 cubed, peeled potatoes (peeling is optional)—the more potatoes, the thicker the soup— and at least 4 cups vegetable or chicken broth. Add any chopped vegetables you want to make it a cream-of-whatever soup, like broccoli, spinach, carrots, or pumpkin. Cook on medium heat till the potatoes are soft. Stir in 1–2 tablespoons of cashew butter. Blend in batches or with an immersion blender till creamy, adding salt and pepper to taste. This soup is cheap and adaptable to whatever you have on hand, and it can be made vegan, vegetarian, and nut free.

# October 18

*"Healing on the causative or primal level necessitates changing the patterns that govern experience, and while most people in pursuit of healing claim to be seeking a state of complete wellness, this depth of healing is typically shied away from."*

Loren Cruden[98]

The above sentence is worth reading a few times. Deep healing requires deep change in the underlying patterns of how we live our lives; such a comprehensive change is often terrifying. While Cruden writes about personal healing, this deep change in pattern also applies to global healing. The reason we as a species haven't completely changed the way we do business on earth—switching completely to clean energy, letting rainforests and swamps flourish, growing organic, etc.—is because to do so would require us to let go of many of our assumptions

about what it means to be human. We have to let go of valuing money for its own sake above all else. Let go of our ideas that we know better than nature. Release our unhealthy masculine ideals of self-as-an-island.

Write today in your journal about Cruden's assertion that most of us shy away from complete wellness and the fear of deep change. How do you see this in yourself?

# October 19

The word *decay* comes from the Latin, meaning "fall down" (*de-cadare*). A fallen log, a fallen soldier, a fallen leaf—all decay in the end. Decay, of course, feeds life: microbes, beetles, flies, ravens, soil, mushrooms.

The underground part of a mushroom is called mycelium. Tear apart a decaying log to find its white, reaching strands. The "flower" grows above ground in order to spread spores. This is the part we eat (or don't eat, as the case may be). Mushrooms are cooling in thermal nature. They reduce fat in the blood (perhaps that's why we eat them with meat) and reduce respiratory mucus. They increase white blood cell count, improve cellular oxygenation, and contain cancer-fighting properties. Paul Pitchford cautions long-time vegans from eating too many mushrooms unless specifically treating disease because they can be *too* cleansing.[99]

Toss some mushrooms on your pizza or salad tonight, or have roasted portabella burgers. Give thanks to the "fallen" life that supported this immune-enhancing fungus.

# October 20

*"Real fearlessness is the product of tenderness.
It comes from letting the world tickle your
heart, your raw and beautiful heart."*
· · · · · · ·
Chögyam Trungpa[100]

Think of the thing or person you love most in the world.
Feel your raw and tender heart as this person or thing
comes to mind. This deep love can sometimes bring
us to cling to this person or thing. But just as a mother
must let her child be free, we love this thing so deeply,
so tenderly, that we let our child (or experience or lover
or forest or...) fly free into the world. *For God so loved the
world...* Then, when we have let our hearts be tickled and
no longer let our deepest fears direct who we are, we
are also truly free. We are fearless. Tender. Strong—and
utterly vulnerable.

Hold these ideas in your heart today like a butterfly in your palm. When do you notice fear? When do

you notice yourself letting go and trusting in love and fearlessness?

## October 21

Make some art with nature today. Arrange autumn leaves by color, floated on a puddle or lined up along a log. Or form spirals out of sticks, shells, or stones. Sand can be sculpted into labyrinths or mandalas and decorated with rocks, fall flowers, dried berries, or whatever else you find. Take a picture of your work when finished, if you like, and leave it for someone else to discover or the wind or waves to disassemble. This is a fun activity with children and adults both. When finished, check out books or videos about Andy Goldsworthy for more inspiration.

## October 22

Has Jack Frost come to play? I still picture a little blue and silver elf tripping in at night and spreading frost upon the grass and window panes, an image formed in my childhood. "Grandfather Frost is the Russian equivalent of Father Christmas," K. M. Sheard tells us in *Llewellyn's Complete Book of Names*.[101] To freeze something is to hold it still in time and space. What is held in stasis for you right now? What is being held in the cleansing cold of approaching winter? Just as life and death balance each other, so do motion and stillness. Reflect today on what is still for you and why.

# October 23

Again plants pull their energy into their roots. It is time for us, too, to ground, to root. Find a place to sit, inside or out, and feel the weight of your bones and flesh being pulled toward the center of the earth. You are of the earth and will be as long as you inhabit this life. Bring to mind images, words, or experiences that have come up over the past year as you moved through these daily devotions. Hold them in your lap: really imagine these words or images sitting in your lap like bubbles of light. Ground them. Just as the trees and shrubs are reaching down into the earth, let your experiences become grounded. See the nutrients of your experiences and discoveries wind and tangle with your own energy. Sit and breathe as your deeply rooted, grounded self.

# October 24

Today the sun enters Scorpio, a sign typified by a remarkable reserve of energy. Scorpio is determined and forceful, powerful and passionate, exciting and magnetic. As we wrap up our devotional year, identify at least three projects you intend to put powerful energy into in the coming year. What has this devotional helped you clarify about your life, your relationship to the earth, and your relationship with Spirit? Take time today to tap into the great power of the sign of Scorpio and to direct that energy toward this clarity and purpose. Write down your projects and goals in your journal or discuss them with a trusted friend.

# October 25

October is known as Falling Leaf Moon (Native American) and Leaf Dance Moon (Druid). Is that appropriate for your climate? If it is, let yourself be a child today. Go play and dance with the leaves. Find a grove of trees and ask it aloud if you may dance. They will probably invite you in. Most trees, I find, respond with warmth and joy when we seek out connection with them. A nice windy day is best, as the leaves pour off the trees and swirl across the earth. Dance with them. Let yourself swirl, fall, and spin. Bring scarves with you to blow in the wind, or wear a long skirt. Allow yourself to fill with joy.

If this doesn't fit your climate, consider what you would call the moon of October. How can you play with this energy?

# October 26

Fall's southward bird migration peaks in October. To attract a large variety of birds to your yard, provide several kinds of feeders. Include a hopper-style feeder with lots of black-oil sunflower and white millet, a ground-style feeder, a suet or peanut block, and a nyjer feeder for finches. Let your bushes and vines grow wild, for the cover will attract and delight birds. Consider getting a de-icer for your bird bath or pond so birds will have access to water even when it freezes. Put the goo and seeds from inside your pumpkins outside on a tray; finches, sparrow, jays, juncos, and squirrels will clean it all up. This is also a good time of year to make another seed block (see February 11) to provide lasting high-calorie food for birds.

## October 27

I took a fall walk in a grove of cottonwoods recently and took a moment to project my awareness into the trees and the land. A wave of sensing the trees' ancestors came over me. The valley had been farmland, and then had been altered by the re-routing of a river. The trees had moved in to line the banks of the new stream. They grew there when planted by the wind, their seeds blown from miles away. They still held the resonance of their parent trees. These trees were aware of their own ancestry. They brought that resonance to the new creek. Along the muddy banks on the far side of the creek we saw prints of deer, raccoon, and beaver, who also now call this previously dry place home.

This communication made me realize the power of relationship. Everything changes, but everything is connected through time and space. It is the unified movement of beauty. Sit today with trees, land, water, stones,

anything, and ask these beings about relationship and ancestry. What do they have to share with you?

# October 28

Today begins the Celtic lunar month of Ngetal, reed. The reed is a symbol of power and royalty, and was the plant from which arrows were cut. It was used in thatching roofs, and "a house is not an established house until the roof is on."[102] Having a roof over one's head gives one a sense of security, and without security, you can't really feel a sense of healthy power. Furthermore, until the roof over your head and other basic needs are taken care of, it's harder to devote energy to movements like saving the planet.

Are your basic needs being cared for? If any are not, what steps can you take to change that? Draw on all you have discovered this year about food, community, and inner resources to address any changes you need to make.

When your needs are met and the roof over your head is solid, consider how you can help others in your

community to do the same. Food pantries, local shelters, and Habitat for Humanity always need volunteers. If you have the time, consider sharing some of your power with them.

# October 29

Some Native Americans refer to the earth's nonhuman animals and plants as "all our relations." Animals in Native culture are seen as beings in their own right, who are related to us as spiritual cousins who share this same, sacred planet. Can you see how this idea of relationship with all is not just a mental construct but a part of the fabric of the universe? Can you feel that connection with trees, stones, the soil, and the rain? We are no longer so alone as a species. We are neither shepherds nor kings. We are in kinship with the earth. How does this change the way you think of the idea of ancestors? As you build your Samhain altar, include some of your nonhuman ancestors in your sacred space.

## October 30

We find ourselves back where we began, on the eve of Samhain. Wrap up your year by writing about how these practices have changed you. What has awakened? What have you released? How has your relationship evolved with Spirit and Earth, God and Goddess, energy and matter?

Read previous journal entries, review your art projects, and reflect on your acts of compassion in the world. Take some time to sit before a candle in silence.

# Suggested Reading

*Medicine Grove: A Shamanic Herbal* by Loren Cruden, 1997.

*Witch Crafting: A Spiritual Guide to Making Magic* by Phyllis Curott, 2001.

*Creation Spirituality: Liberating Gifts for the Peoples of the Earth* by Matthew Fox, 1991.

*Medicine for the Earth* and *How to Thrive in Changing Times* by Sandra Ingerman, 2001 and 2010.

*The Nature Principle: Reconnecting with Life in a Virtual Age* by Richard Louv, 2012.

*Coming Back to Life: Practices to Reconnect Our Lives, Our World* by Joanna Macy and Molly Young Brown, 1998.

*Nature and the Human Soul: Cultivating Wholeness and Community in a Fragmented World* by Bill Plotkin, 2007.

*Earth Prayers From Around the World: 365 Prayers, Poems, and Invocations for Honoring the Earth* by Elizabeth Roberts and Elias Amidon, 2009.

*The Universe Story: From the Primordial Flaring Forth to the Ecozoic Era—A Celebration of the Unfolding of the Cosmos* by Brian Swimme and Thomas Berry, 1992.

I also include even more practices in my books *Sacred Land* and *Voices of the Earth*.

# Endnotes

1    J. J. Bachofen, *Myth, Religion, and Mother Right*, trans. Ralph Manheim, Bollingen Series 84 (Princeton University Press, 1976), 34. Quoted in Barbara G. Walker, *The Women's Encyclopedia of Myths and Secrets* (New York: HarperSanFrancisco, 1983), 215.

2    Dianne Sylvan, *The Circle Within: Creating a Wiccan Spiritual Practice* (St Paul: Llewellyn Publications, 2004), 29.

3    Paul Pitchford, *Healing with Whole Foods: Oriental Tradition and Modern Medicine* (Berkley, CA: North Atlantic Books, 1993), 307.

4    Bill Plotkin, *Soulcraft: Crossing into the Mysteries of Nature and Psyche* (Novato, CA: New World Library, 2003), 135.

5    Matthew Fox, *Creation Spirituality: Liberating Gifts for the Peoples of the Earth* (New York: Harper Collins, 1991), 18.

6    Bill Plotkin, *Nature and the Human Soul: Cultivating Wholeness and Community in a Fragmented World* (Novato, CA: New World Library, 2008), 238.

7    Susun Weed, *Healing Wise: A Wise Woman Herbal* (Woodstock, NY: Ash Tree Publishing, 1989), 16.

8    Michael S. Schneider, *A Beginner's Guide to Constructing the Universe: The Mathematical Archetypes of Nature, Art, and Science* (New York: Harper Perennial, 1994), xxii.

9    Masaru Emoto, *Messages from Water and the Universe* (Carlsbad, CA: Hay House, 2010), 67.

10    Martin Chaplin, *Water Structure and Science*, http://www.lsbu.ac.uk/water/anmlies.html.

11    Caroline Myss, *Defy Gravity: Healing Beyond the Bounds of Reason* (Carlsbad, CA: Hay House, 2009), 117.

12    Satish Kumar, "Soil, Soul, and Society," a TED talk published April 30, 2012, at http://www.youtube.com/watch?v=uSLUdoveioU.

13    Phoenix McFarland, *The Complete Book of Magical Names* (St. Paul, MN: Llewellyn Publications, 1999), 119.

14    Ibid., 119.

15    Ursula K. Le Guin, *Buffalo Gals and Other Animal Presences* (New York: Penguin, 1987), 196.

16    Loren Cruden, *Medicine Grove: A Shamanic Herbal* (Rochester, VT: Destiny Books, 1997), 61.

17    Bill McKibben, *Eaarth: Making a Life on a Tough New Planet* (New York: St. Martin's Griffin, 2010), 15.

18    The Findhorn Community, *The Findhorn Garden Story* (Forred, Scotland: Findhorn Press, 1975, 2008).

19    Jamie Sams and David Carson, *Medicine Cards: The Discovery of Power Through the Ways of Animals* (Santa Fe: Bear & Co., 1988), 121.

20    Philip and Stephanie Carr-Gomm, *The Druid Animal Oracle: Working with the Sacred Animals of the Druid Tradition* (New York: Simon & Schuster, 1994), 50.

21    D. J. Conway, *Magic of the Gods and Goddesses* (Berkley, CA: The Crossing Press, 2003), 243.

22    Sams and Carson, *Medicine Cards*, 41.

23    McFarland, *The Complete Book of Magical Names*, 119.

24    Anne Schmauss, Mary Schmauss, and Geni Klolick, *For the Birds: A Month-by-Month Guide to Attracting Birds to Your Backyard* (New York: Stewart, Tabori, & Chang, 2008), 49.

25    Jim Marion, *Putting on the Mind of Christ: The Inner Work of Christian Spirituality* (Charlottesville, VA: Hampton Roads, 2000), 163.

26    Cruden, *Medicine Grove*, 5.

27  Brian Swimme and Thomas Berry, *The Universe Story: From the Primordial Flaring Forth to the Ecozoic Era* (New York: Harper San Francisco, 1992), 8.

28  "Native American Names," Goddard Space Flight Center, online at http://imagine.gsfc.nasa.gov/docs/ask_astro /answers/970314a.html.

29  "February," Online Etymology Dictionary, http://www .etymonline.com.

30  "The Bitter Truth About Chocolate," http://www.treehugger .com/green-food/the-bitter-truth-about-chocolate.html.

31  Institute of Heart Math, "The Energetic Heart Is Unfolding," http://www.heartmath.org/templates /ihm/e-newsletter/article/2010/summer/energetic -heart-is-unfolding.php.

32  Anne Underwood, "For a Happy Heart," *Newsweek*, 9/27/2004, vol. 144, issue 13, 54.

33  Sams and Carson, *Medicine Cards*, 65–66.

34  "February," *Encyclopædia Britannica 1911*, http://en.wikisource .org/wiki/1911_Encyclop%C3%A6dia_Britannica/February.

35  Cruden, *Medicine Grove*, 42.

36  Ibid., 69.

37  Marion, *Putting on the Mind of Christ*, 163.

38  "The Plum Blossom: A Symbol of Strength," *The Epoch Times*,
    www.theepochtimes.com.

39  www.therapycolor.com.

40  As quoted in *The Earth Speaks: An Acclimatization Journal*,
    ed. Steve van Matre and Bill Weiler (Greenville, WV:
    The Institute for Earth Education, 1983), 13.

41  All astrological information is from Julia and Derek Parker,
    *Parkers' Astrology: The Definitive Guide to Using Astrology in Every
    Aspect of Your Life* (New York: DK Publishing, 1994).

42  Deanna Caswell and Daisy Siskin, *Little House in the
    Suburbs: Backyard Farming and Home Skills for Self-Sufficient Living*
    (Cincinnati, OH: Betterway Home, 2012), 170–171.

43  Ly de Angeles, Emma Restall Orr, Thom van Doreen, et. al.,
    *Pagan Visions for a Sustainable Future* (Woodbury, MN: Llewellyn,
    2005), 257.

44  Thom van Doreen, *Pagan Visions for a Sustainable Future*, 260.

45  Jeanne E. Arnold, Anthony P. Graesch, Enzo Ragazzini,
    and Elinor Ochs, *Life at Home in the Twenty-First Century* (Los
    Angeles: Cotsen Institute of Archaeology, 2012).

46  Fox, *Creation Spirituality*, 18.

47  Ibid, 19.

48 Kahlil Gibran, quoted in *The Earth Speaks: An Acclimatization Journal*, ed. Steve van Matre and Bill Weiler (Greenville, WV: The Institute for Earth Education, 1983), 40.

49 Stanley Kunitz, *The Wild Braid: A Poet Reflects on a Century in the Garden* (New York: W. W. Norton & Co., 2005), 13.

50 Fox, *Creation Spirituality*, 19.

51 Swimme and Berry, *The Universe Story*, 54.

52 Graham Bell, *The Permaculture Garden* (White River Junction, VT: Chelsea Green Publishing Co., 2004), 137.

53 Don Cornis, "Settling Doubts About Livestock Stress," *Agricultural Research*, March 2005, vol. 53, issue 3, 5.

54 Weed, *Healing Wise*, 158.

55 Burleigh Mutén, *Godesses: A World of Myth and Magic* (Cambridge, MA: Barefoot Books, 2003), 75.

56 Phyllis Curott, *Witch Crafting: A Spiritual Guide to Making Magic* (New York: Broadway Books, 2001), 313.

57 Fox, *Creation Spirituality*, 21.

58 Alan Gussow, "A Sense of Place," quoted in *The Earth Speaks: An Acclimatization Journal*, ed. Steve van Matre and Bill Weiler, (Greenville, WV: The Institute for Earth Education, 1983), 45.

59 Ibid.

60   Daniel Chamovitz, *What a Plant Knows: A Field Guide to the Senses* (New York: Scientific American/Farrar, Straus and Giroux, 2012), 6.

61   Curott, *Witch Crafting*, 141.

62   "Native American Names," Goddard Space Flight Center, http://imagine.gsfc.nasa.gov/docs/ask_astro /answers/970314a.html.

63   Emma Restall Orr, "Unit Seven: Field Poppy Moon," *A Perennial Course in Living Druidry*, http://druidnetwork.org /en/learning/courses/online/perennial/unit7.

64   *The Singing Creek Where the Willows Grow*, quoted in Catriona MacGregor, *Partnering with Nature: The Wild Path to Reconnecting with the Earth* (New York: Atria/Simon & Schuster, 2010), 175.

65   Jessica McMaken, personal email to the author, August 29, 2012.

66   Richard Louv, "The Family Nature Club," *The Nature Principle: Human Restoration and the End of Nature-Deficit Disorder* (Chapel Hill, NC: Algonquin Books, 2011), 149.

67   Robert Krulwich, "Look Up! The Billion-Bug Highway You Can't See," online blog at http://www.npr.org/blogs /krulwich/2011/06/01/128389587/look-up-the-billion -bug-highway-you-cant-see.

68   Louv, *The Nature Principle*, 61.

69  Kunitz, *The Wild Braid*, 62.

70  Ellen Dugan, "Crafty Crafts," in *Llewellyn's Sabbats Almanac,*
    Samhain 2011 to Mabon 2012 (Woodbury, MN: Llewellyn
    Worldwide, 2011), 220–221.

71  Ben Good, "Amphibious houses float out of trouble in
    Bangladesh," http://www.scidev.net/en/news/amphibious
    -houses-float-out-of-trouble-in-bangladesh.html.

72  Clea Danaan, *Sacred Land: Intuitive Gardening for Personal, Political
    & Environmental Change* (Woodbury, MN: Llewellyn, 2007),
    168.

73  Plotkin, *Nature and the Human Soul*, 162–163.

74  Most sources site this as "author unknown," but I did find
    one attribution to Earthdance at http://www.sparkcollective.
    org/node/28. This could be the yearly Pagan gathering or a
    person called Earthdance.

75  Fox, *Creation Spirituality*, 23.

76  Myss, *Defy Gravity*, 9.

77  Adapted from a quote by James Finley in Caroline Myss, *Defy
    Gravity*, 40.

78  "The Day Out of Time," http://www.13moon.com/doot.htm.

79  Plotkin, *Nature and the Human Soul*, 318–320.

80  Ibid., 224.

81  Pitchford, *Healing with Whole Foods*, 299.

82  Ibid., 504–505.

83  Plotkin, *Soulcraft*, 39.

84  Gary Oppenheimer, "AmpleHarvest.org" a TED talk dated January 21, 2012, viewed online at http://www.ampleharvest .org/LTEDx-view.php.

85  Pitchford, *Healing with Whole Foods*, 425.

86  Online at http://www.reuters.com/article/2012/08/10 /usa-crops-idUSL2E8JA3NT20120810.

87  Curott, *Witch Crafting*, 69.

88  Shanon Sinn, "Muin (Grape Vine)," *The Living Library*, published on July 13, 2011, http://livinglibraryblog .com/?p=149.

89  Bell, *The Permaculture Garden*, 150.

90  Susan W. Madsen and Tim Nightengale, "Whatcom Creek Post-Fire Evaluation—10 Years After," City of Bellingham Department of Public Works, May 29, 2009.

91  Quoted in Kenny Ausubel, *Restoring the Earth: Visionary Solutions from the Bioneers* (Tiburon, CA: H. J. Kramer, 1997), 101.

92  Sharon Palmer, "Microgreens Become a Macro Trend to Follow," *Environmental Nutrition*, June 2010, vol. 33, issue 6, 8.

93   "Why Drink Organic Wine," http://www.turangacreek.co.nz/buying-organic-wine/.

94   McFarland, *The Complete Book of Magical Names*, 114.

95   Quoted by Leah Piken Kolidas in her blog "Creative Every Day," posted September 26, 2009, at http://creativeeveryday.com/creativeeveryday/2009/09/creative-every-day-challenge-theme-for-october-connect.html.

96   Sams and Carson, *Medicine Cards*.

97   Carr-Gomm, *The Druid Animal Oracle*, 66.

98   Cruden, *Medicine Grove*, 4.

99   Pitchford, *Healing with Whole Foods*, 502.

100  Chögyam Trungpa, *Shambhala: The Sacred Path of the Warrior* (Boston: Shambhala, 1988), 46.

101  K. M. Sheard, *Llewellyn's Complete Book of Names* (Woodbury, MN: Llewellyn Worldwide, 2011), 238.

102  Robert Graves, *The White Goddess* (New York: Farrar, Straus, and Giroux, 1974), 185.

# GET MORE AT **LLEWELLYN.COM**

Visit us online to browse hundreds of our books and decks, plus sign up to receive our e-newsletters and exclusive online offers.

- **Free tarot readings • Spell-a-Day • Moon phases**
- **Recipes, spells, and tips • Blogs • Encyclopedia**
- **Author interviews, articles, and upcoming events**

# GET SOCIAL WITH **LLEWELLYN**

**Find us on**
**Facebook**
www.Facebook.com/LlewellynBooks

**Follow us on**
**twitter**
www.Twitter.com/Llewellynbooks

# GET BOOKS AT **LLEWELLYN**

## LLEWELLYN ORDERING INFORMATION

**Order online:** Visit our website at www.llewellyn.com to select your books and place an order on our secure server.

**Order by phone:**
- Call toll free within the U.S. at 1-877-NEW-WRLD (1-877-639-9753)
- Call toll free within Canada at 1-866-NEW-WRLD (1-866-639-9753)
- We accept VISA, MasterCard, and American Express

**Order by mail:**
Send the full price of your order (MN residents add 6.875% sales tax) in U.S. funds, plus postage and handling to: Llewellyn Worldwide, 2143 Wooddale Drive Woodbury, MN 55125-2989

**POSTAGE AND HANDLING**

STANDARD (U.S. & Canada):
(Please allow 12 business days)
$25.00 and under, add $4.00.
$25.01 and over, FREE SHIPPING.

INTERNATIONAL ORDERS (airmail only):
$16.00 for one book, plus $3.00 for each additional book.

Visit us online for more shipping options.
Prices subject to change.

## FREE CATALOG!

To order, call
1-877-
NEW-WRLD
ext. 8236
or visit our
website

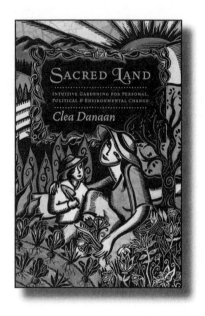

To order, call 1-877-NEW-WRLD

*Prices subject to change without notice*

Order at llewellyn.com 24 hours a day, 7 days a week!

# Sacred Land
### Intuitive Gardening for Personal, Political & Environmental Change

## *Clea Danaan*

Clea Danaan breaks new ground with *Sacred Land*—a fresh approach to sacred gardening that goes beyond the backyard.

Danaan shows how the garden can germinate environmental awareness and political change while feeding the spirit. You'll learn how to create compost, save seeds, connect with garden goddesses, perform rituals and magic, and incorporate planetary energy in the garden. Each of the four sections—spanning earth, air, fire, and water—suggest ways of spreading this message of ecology and sustainability to the community. There are also inspiring stories of activists, farmers, artists, healers, and other women who are making a difference in the world.

*978-0-7387-1146-1*
*$15.95 · 5³⁄₁₆ x 8 · 288 pp.*